Sketches of California in the 1860s

THE JOURNALS OF JESUS M. ESTUDILLO

Edited and Annotated by
Margaret Schlichtmann

Awani Press

ISBN 0–915266–18–0

First Printing

Contents

Illustrations

Foreword

Few places on the face of the earth have changed more in the last century and a half than the San Francisco Bay Area. Barren, wind-swept hills have given way to high-rise apartments and office buildings; cattle grazing on vast East Bay *ranchos* have been replaced by wall-to-wall houses; and roads on which stagecoaches sank to their hubs and horses to their bellies in dust or mud, depending on the season, now are high-speed expressways.

To describe the way it was Margaret Schlichtmann has edited the diaries of a young *Californio,* Jesus Maria Estudillo, writen in the 1860s. These describe family life at his *Rancho San Leandro* home, plus sketches of San Francisco, Oakland, San Jose and Santa Clara, and a steamer trip to Southern California. His happy times, trials and tribulations as an undergraduate at Santa Clara University are told in some detail.

To Estudillo's diary Mrs. Schlichtmann has added her own notes, describing places and events in more detail, with excerpts from such prominent writers of the day as William H. Brewer, R. H. Dana, Jr. and J. Ross Brown. References to place names used today and descriptions of animal and plant life as it used to be from these keen observers are of equal interest to Estudillo's writing.

The combination of Estudillo and Schlichtmann—he describing the life of his time, problems such as his family's loss of much of their East Bay land grant to squatters and to litigation following the Gold Rush, and troubles resulting from the Civil War—she adding notes from careful observation and research a century later make this book of value to anyone interested in California history.

We are pleased to add it to a companion volume by Mrs. Schlichtmann and Irene Paden, *The Big Oak Flat Road to Yosemite,* which won the Commonwealth Club award for the greatest contribution to California history the year it was published.

The Awani Press
Fredericksburg, Texas 78624

Jesus Maria Estudillo in his 30's

Scene near San Leandro in the 1880's

Preface and Acknowledgements

Young men of eighteen are not apt to record their personal experiences for the benefit of future history-minded individuals or the curious. Jesus Maria Estudillo's "Strictly Private" *Journal for 1862* was written during his first year as a boarding student at Santa Clara College, the present University nestled in California's scenic and historic Santa Clara Valley.

The diarist was born on Rancho San Leandro on June 29, 1844; the eleventh and last child of Don Jose Joaquin Estudillo and his wife, the former Senorita Juana Maria del Carmen Martinez. For a decade, beginning in 1836, the generally peaceful life of his parents and other upper-class Californios was indeed in contrast to the political and revolutionary upheavals throughout Alta California. This period of changes and uncertainties continued until 1848 when the Stars and Stripes replaced the Mexican colors. Despite the change in government and the incursion of strangers from other lands, the Estudillos continued their pastoral way of life and clung tenaciously to customs of old Spain.

The unprecedented Gold Rush, followed by California's statehood on September 9, 1850, brought changes causing the family to relinquish complacency and accept American laws and customs. This, however, did not affect the childhood of Jesus Maria. He experienced his first great sorrow at the age of eight upon the death of his father who had already been confronted with perplexing problems upon the infiltration of squatters on his Mexican grant.

Jesus Maria was enrolled as a boarding student in the preparatory department of Santa Clara College in September, 1856. Although he discontinued his formal education in 1864, without obtaining a degree (not uncommon in the 19th Century), he was well educated. At the end of each semester, the Jesuit Fathers commended him for his diligence, politeness, faithful attendance to all religious services and his unwavering compliance to the exacting rules of the institution.

In preference to attaining wealth or prominence in the business world, the young man decided on a simple way of life, close ties with his family, the experience of attending great operas and the reading of classics. ". . . for with my dear books, I can always find a world of pleasure."

Jesus Maria kept diaries from January, 1861, through 1867, but to date, only his journals of 1861, '62, '64, and 1867 have been discovered.

A brief account of Jesus Maria's ancestors, heritage and environment preceeds the editing of *Journal for 1862,* but to record all the trials and military assignments of his maternal and paternal grandfathers during the Spanish and Mexican Periods, would expand these chapters beyond a reasonable limit. Space does not permit details of the Estudillos' struggle to retain Rancho San Leandro and have it finally patented by the U.S. Government.

Excerpts from the works of J. Ross Browne, Reverend Walter Colton, Benjamin I. Hayes and William H. Brewer enable one to envision Jesus Maria Estudillo in San Francisco, Benicia, Sacramento, at Santa Clara College and in southern California. *Journal for 1862* exhibits his high moral principles, sensitive nature and controlled deportment. Despite his family's prominence and social status, Jesus Maria was in part a lonely, frustrated lad whose pride and sensitivity is manifested through his journal.

The author of this dissertation extends heartfelt gratitude to relatives and friends of Jesus Maria Estudillo, most of whom are now at rest, but whose reminiscences made it possible to give more than a shadowy characterization of the eighteen-year old diarist. I am also deeply indebted to other friends for their cooperation, interest and encouragement during my laborious, yet gratifying research to do justice to the subject. Most worthy are the late Mr. James D. Forward, President of the Union Title and Insurance Company of San Diego; the late Director and Mrs. W. Edwin Gledhill of the Santa Barbara Historical Society; Mrs. Helen Rocca Goss, also of Santa Barbara and author of commendable additions to Californiana; and to Dr. George F. Hammond, historian of note and Director Emeritus of the Bancroft Library at the University of California, Berkeley, California. Gratitude is also extended to Miss Ruth

I. Mahood, Chief Curator of the History Division of the Los Angeles County Museum, whose gracious guidance enabled me to uncover valuable historical data. Profound gratitude is due to the late Reverend Father Arthur D. Spearman, S.J., then Historian and Chief Archivist of the University of Santa Clara, and to Mr. William H. Oliver, formerly of Rancho Santa Fe in San Diego County who assisted in locating parts of the ancient *Camino Real*.

Not to be overlooked is my genial and cooperative husband, Emil, who patiently accompanied me on repeated journeys along the coastal regions of California in search of data pertaining to my project. His deep appreciation of nature's wonders, interest in adobe ruins, remaining historical structures and the course of the early Padres from Mission Santo Tomas in Mexico to the most northerly of California's missions made for treasured memories.

Margaret Schlichtmann

Editor's Note: Due to an illness of long duration, Margaret Schlichtmann was unable to complete this publication. Her husband, Emil, asked my assistance in completing the manuscript which required editing and updating. My special thanks and acknowledgement are extended to Emil, to Father Gerald McKevitt, S.J., Director, University Archives, University of Santa Clara, and to Julia O'Keefe, Assistant Archivist. Last but not least, to Loretta Tulley, who provided me with immense help in final editing and typing.

Marie Wilson

1

Jesus Maria Estudillo
Ancestors and Family

Two hours before midnight on June 29, 1844, a baby boy arrived with exceptionally large dark eyes like those of his handsome father. A mission record reads: "In the Church of this Mission San Jose, on the 11th day of November 1844, the Reverend Father Muro baptized solemnly a little boy born on the 29th of June of the same year and gave him the name of Jesus Maria of the Trinity. He is the legitimate son of Joaquin Estudillo and Juana Martinez; his godparents were Victor Castro and Guadalupe Moraga to whom I gave notice of their responsibilities in the matter and signed below, Fray Jose de Jesus Gutierrez."

The year marked the eve of California's turbulent and political existence. The child was one of eleven born to Juana and Jose Joaquin Estudillo.

The founder of California's Estudillo families was Jose Maria Estudillo y Gomez, a native of Antequera in the province of Andalucia in Spain. Estudillo joined the Spanish military forces in *Nueva Espana* (Mexico) on July 23, 1796, and for a short period served as a cadet in the Loreto Presidio company in Lower California. [H.H. Bancroft, *Pioneer Register,* Vol. II, p. 542.] Here he married Ana Maria Gertrudis Orcasitas y Herrera, a native of Tlayacapa in the Archdiocese of Mexico City. [Carmel Mission Baptismal Records, Vol. 1, Entry 2279, June 11, 1799.] By the year 1799, Estudillo was stationed at the Royal Presidio of San Carlos de Monterey in Alta California, on an almost barren rise overlooking the bay and enclosed by a high adobe wall.

At that time, living at the Monterey post was exceedingly primitive.

1

Four years later, substantial barracks and dwellings for officers and their families replaced the crude, earlier structures. Despite these improvements, it remained a weak defensive outpost with less than one hundred poorly equipped troops and a minimum of weapons.

On May 5, 1800, Maria Gertrudis Estudillo bore a healthy boy. Two days later, he was placed in the care of his appointed godparents to be baptized at Mission Carmel. Here, Fray Jacinto Lopez named the child *Joaquin Antonio Jose Ygnacio Fernando Ramon Pio V.* The last name was given in honor of Pio Quinto or Pope Pius V., the Pontiff of the Battle of Lepanto in 1571. Because baptismal names of that period were exceedingly lengthy, children were frequently known by only two names chosen from the baptismal record. The Estudillos chose *Jose Joaquin* for their first son, who later became grantee of Rancho San Leandro and the father of diarist, Jesus Maria.

Spain had neglected California for 166 years after Vizcaino's voyages along the coast in 1602 and 1603. Then in 1769, determined to colonize the strange land, neither the Spanish Crown nor its representatives in Mexico fully appreciated the hardships that were thrust upon the Franciscans in the military forces. Once the missions were established, Alta California was again forgotten. Conditions worsened after 1811 owing to Mexico's profound determination to free itself of the Spanish yoke. Spanish vessels avoided California's harbors in fear of privateers. By 1820, Spain had lost her position as the world's wealthiest and most powerful nation and was faced with the grave possibility of being forced to relinquish Mexico which, since the days of Cortez, had provided gold for her treasury.

In 1822, Jose Maria Estudillo received orders to take command of the Santa Barbara Presidio, where he continued until his death on April 8, 1830. [Bancroft's Works, Vol. II, p. 542.] According to H.H. Bancroft, Estudillo's vanity and other objectionable characteristics were thoroughly disliked by the troops and other officers. [*Ibid.*, pp. 538, 540.] However, his faults were considered minor by the military leaders in Mexico, who upon orders from Spain, were to select only men of good character to fulfill important presidial duties. Jose Maria Estudillo was a faithful officer but colorless compared to our diarist's maternal grandfather, Ygnacio Martinez de la Vega. Estudillo did not leave an estate; however, had he lived during the secularization of California's missions (1834-1837), he undoubtedly would have been awarded mission acreage for his fearless participation in Indian uprisings and other military services.

Ygnacio Martinez de la Vega was born in Mexico City in 1774, the second son of Antonio Martinez and his wife, Maria Manuela de la Vega. [J.M. Estudillo, Biographical Notes, undated.] Despite his father's prominence among military leaders in Spain and Mexico, neither Ygnacio not his elder brother, Antonio, were attracted by the glamour of uniforms or adventure. Ygnacio was studying for the priesthood at the Apostolic College of San Fernando de Mexico in Mexico City, where his brother was already a Friar, when he decided to change his course in life. [*Ibid.*] Our diarist wrote: ". . . One day, while studying in the garden, he allowed his thoughts to wander from his books to the pleasures of the world. He determined suddenly to give up the church. He at once took off his cassock, hung it in a tree and scaled the wall, thereby gaining his liberty and as soon as possible thereafter, joined the army." [*Ibid.*] This took place in 1799, when Ygnacio joined the Spanish military forces in Mexico City.

Early 1805 found Martinez, his wife and their two year old daughter [personal interviews with the late Elice Cushing and Lilly Davis], living at the Santa Barbara Presidio, where on March 30, Maria Marina Arellanes de Martinez gave birth to another daughter. She was baptized *Juana Maria del Carmen* and later became the mother of Jesus Maria Estudillo, the diarist. [J.M. Estudillo, *Journey for 1867.*] Juana Maria was still a babe in arms when her father was ordered back to the Santa Barbara Presidio.

Soon after their arrival, Martinez was informed that by some error made in Spain or Mexico, he was instead to serve at *El Castillo de San Joaquin,* the latter the San Francisco Presidio and not in Santa Barbara. [Bancroft's Works, Vol. IV, p. 733. Bancroft states that *El Castillo de San Joaquin* was established in 1794 to offset a threat from the British, represented by Captain George Vancouver.] Because this was a bitter disappointment, Martinez deliberately delayed his departure, but on August 1, 1819, he was finally forced to leave for the northern post. [Grace Carmel Martinez, *op. cit.*] Two more children had been added to the family.

When Martinez arrived at the San Francisco Presidio, the original wooden structures had been replaced by adobes constructed in a quadrangle. However, owing to a series of earthquakes and to poor construction, water often seeped through the adobe walls during the rainy season. The Commandancia or headquarters, which also served as living quarters for the family, was located at the north end of the post, near a cliff edging the southern shore of the strait presently known as the Golden Gate. A small cannon faced the entrance of San Francisco Bay, but was to be fired only by the commander of the post. [W.H. Davis, *Sixty Years In California*.]

Because contact with foreign vessels was prohibited by the Spanish Crown, the scarcity of necessities added to the hardships of Presidio life. After 1815, conditions became so acute that, in order to relieve the plight of the Californios, port officials were finally forced to impose a limited interference with coastal vessels and to overlook a reasonable amount of illegal transit. Dictated by necessity, some trading took place with the Russian colonies north of the San Francisco Presidio, but whenever their vessels moved southward, they were viewed with suspicion. Distrust in Russian maneuvers was especially prevalent at the Monterey Presidio. In 1817, the diarist's paternal grandfather, Jose Maria Estudillo, was accredited with having commanded a party of thirteen men from preventing seven Russian fishing vessels to land at Monterey. Mission Carmel Baptismal Records, Vol. 1, Entry 2812, April 24, 1811, states that Dona Gertrudis Orcasitas, wife of Lt. Jose Maria Estudillo became the godmother of a young Indian woman "from one of the Russian forts." Because she was near death, she was rebaptized and named *Maria Dolores Columba*. [Pages 610 to 626 of W.H. Davis' *Sixty Years in California* lists the names of Russian vessels that entered the port of present San Francisco from 1806 to 1842.]

The conflict resulted in the death of several Russians and the capture of another [Bancroft's Works, Vol. 1, p. 542], whose only intent may have been to take on fresh water and gather firewood.

In November 1822, while serving as Lieutenant of the Cavalry, Ygnacio Martinez was placed in command of the San Francisco Presidio upon Comandante Don Luis Antonio Arguello's appointment to serve as Governor *ad interim* of Alta California. Because the appointment was only provisional, Arguello retained nominally the command of the post. Arguello undoubtedly deemed his appointment as Governor an honor, but also appreciated the insecurity of the assignment. Mexico had freed herself of the Spanish yoke on September 21, 1821, but the duration of her independence remained doubtful owing to Spain's refusal to acknowledge total defeat and release the Spaniards of their fealty.

Arguello was well aware of the jealousies and discord among Mexico's ambitious politicians and military leaders which was apt to affect the governmental affairs of Alta California. Many Mexicans and some Californios found difficulty in adjusting themselves to the new order, or still favored Spanish rule. It was hoped that conditions in California would improve under Mexican colors. In fact they only deteriorated. The depletion of Mexico's wealth and resources during the previous eleven years of bitter warfare impaired the support of the provincial government and of the long-neglected presidios. The gravity of this situation also concerned *Comandante* Martinez. Fort Ross, Russia's largest base for fur hunting expeditions, now had about 300 inhabitants and ample weapons to establish another coastal colony between the sixty odd miles that separated their colony from the San Francisco Presidio.

Among the upper-class Californios, lengthy betrothals were obligatory. In late 1822, the main topic of conversation among the officers' wives was the impending marriage of Juana Maria del Carmen Martinez to Don Jose Joaquin Estudillo. Prior to his transfer to the San Francisco post in 1816, he had served as a cadet at the Monterey Presidio to which he had been assigned when he joined the Spanish military forces in 1815. Although their engagement had been formally announced many months previously, Estudillo, as all officers, was obliged to wait for the marriage permit from headquarters in Mexico. On February 6, 1823, Fray Tomas Estenaga joined the happy couple in holy matrimony. [Mission San Francisco de Assisi (Dolores) Marriage Records, Vol. 1, Entry 1993, February 6, 1823.]

In the following year (1824), Estudillo resigned from military service to become one of Arguello's aides during this chaotic period of governmental affairs in Alta California. By 1827, living conditions at the San Francisco Presidio had declined to such an extent, that the entire garrison was forced to wear moccasin-type shoes made by the neophytes at Mission Dolores. In Fray Zephyrin Engelhardt's *Mission Dolores*, we read that in the spring of 1806, a measles epidemic took over 230 lives within a period of two months. By 1826, the neophyte population had risen to 850. Prior to secularization, over 5000 neophytes at Mission Dolores were given Christian funerals. [*Bay of San Francisco—A History*, Vol. 1, p. 91.]

Officers and troops had been without saddles since 1824, although English and American trading enterprises had increased during Arguello's term as acting-governor of Alta California (1822-1825).

Despite the arrival of trading vessels engaged in illegal trade, neither troops nor the poorly paid officers could afford to purchase luxuries or even necessities.

Because of insurrections in Mexico and the lamentable state of Mexico's treasury, she was forced to levy taxes upon the Californios and missions to support the provincial government. The Franciscans objected strenuously, deeming that their establishments were purely of a religious and educational nature and that they had not been set up by Mexico, but by the Spanish Crown. Then, when Mexico thrust the support of the presidios upon the padres, it was regarded as an added injustice. Mission Dolores, with its greatly reduced neophyte population, already was having difficulties in meeting the demands of the San Francisco post. One wonders how women and children lived under these trying conditions, especially in 1829, when the garrison, owing to insufficient food and clothing, revolted.

April 8, 1830, marked the death of Captain Jose Maria Estudillo and on the following day, he was laid to rest under the earthen floor of the chapel at the San Diego Presidio.

In September 1831, *Comandante* Ygnacio Martinez retired from military service, whereupon Lt. Mariano Guadalupe Vallejo, then about twenty-four years of age, was acting commander of the San Francisco Presidio. Many years later, our diarist, J.M. Estudillo wrote in his notes that his maternal grandfather ". . . retired at full pay and was allowed to wear his uniform, which privilege was rarely granted" [J.M. Estudillo, Biographical Notes, undated], and that after Martinez' death in 1848, each of his children received a silver teaspoon made from the epaulets of his uniform. By early 1832, the Martinez family were living in the Pueblo of San Jose de Guadalupe where Martinez served as a member of the *Ayuntamiento* or City Council.

After more than a decade of presidial life, the Estudillos welcomed living outside the walls of a military establishment, despite the ugliness of the settlement and the ever-prevalent stench of horses and oxen. At that time, Missions Santa Clara and San Jose were at the peak of their prosperity and although living conditions in San Jose were not entirely favorable, food was plentiful. While its inhabitants were enjoying ample quantities of meat, fresh fruits and vegetables, Comandante Vallejo, at the San Francisco Presidio was complaining to Governor Figueroa about conditions at the post; that it was in great destitution mainly because Mission Dolores failed to supply sufficient food for the garrison.

[On page 206 of *San Francisco or Mission Dolores,* Fray Zephyrin Engelhardt declared that Vallejo's complaints were unfounded.] Although the complaint was of concern to the governor, it was less disturbing than a forthcoming event that was to affect all of Alta California's religious establishments.

Although the Mexican Government authorized the secularization of California's twenty-one missions in 1824, it was several years before the wheels of conversion were put into motion. By 1836, the transformation was well under way, although Jose Figueroa had previously counseled the Mexican Government not to adopt the measure. This was in part because he foresaw the hardships that would be thrust upon the neophytes and feared that by releasing them from the jurisdiction of the padres, some, if not all, would resort to their primitive way of life. He also reminded Mexico that the support of the provincial government and the presidios depended mainly upon the missions and that secularization would only add to the plight of the Californios. [Fray Zephyrin Engelhardt, *op. cit.,* pp. 212, 219.] Following the tangled threads of secularization and the policies of Mexico is difficult at best.

Upon Mexico's determination to enforce the decree, Figueroa suggested gradual secularization, but in April 1834, a supplemental law was passed demanding that all missions were to be secularized within four months. [*Ibid.*] In the beginning, only a few of the sacred chapels were converted to parish churches and some Franciscans were returned to Mexico or to their native Spain. Those who were permitted to remain were now subject to the Archbishop of Mexico in spiritual matters and in temporal matters to the governors of Alta California.

Shortly after Mexico demanded that all missions were to be secularized within four months, Jose Joaquin Estudillo and his father-in-law, Ygnacio Martinez were assigned to the complicated procedure of secularizing California's two most northerly missions. Mexico had warned against wanton destruction of mission properties, and demanded that libraries, sacred vessels and furniture be left in care of the remaining padres. Grain was to remain undisturbed and the neophytes, who were to receive their usual rations, were not to be mistreated by colonists. Although they were not entirely subjected, they were not entirely free and were not permitted to establish communities of their own on former mission properties. Comisionados were also to care for the sick. If Estudillo had any degree of compassion, his task at Mission Dolores must have been especially trying. The most revolting and pitiful ailments among the Indians had been acquired by association with the lowest class of troops from the San Francisco Presidio who had defied orders not to leave the post except when assigned to military duties.

The period of secularization is considered by many the most unjust and ugliest in the annals of California. Rev. Walter Colton wrote: "The civil administrators plundered them of their stock, the governors granted to favorites sections of their land, until with few exceptions, only huge buildings remain." [Rev. Walter Colton, *Three Years in California*, p. 440.] Don Mariano Vallejo, who with his brother Salvador, held princely estates in present Sonoma County, stated that these accusations were absurd. [W.H. Davis, *op. cit.*, p. 475.] He and other recipients of mission properties, including Estudillo, had been accused of misdeeds during this period of turmoil and hasty onslaughts by jealous rivals. Vallejo favored secularization. Many, many years later he said: "I have rejoiced from the bottom of my heart at the liberation of these poor people from the clutches of the missionaries." [*Ibid.*] This bitter statement may derive from Vallejo's difficulties with the padres and Garcia Diego, California's first Bishop of the Roman Catholic Church. However, Vallejo never rejected Catholicism. It remains doubtful if these "poor people", who after their liberation, served as vaqueros and servants on Vallejo's and other princely estates, fared any better than they had in the "clutches of the missionaries." [*Ibid.*]

In May, 1835, Governor Figueroa started a small settlement about three miles east and somewhat north of Mission Dolores. In June of the same year (1835), Ygnacio Martinez' son-in-law, William A. Richardson, an Englishman by birth, built the first habitation in San Francisco other than the structures at the presidio and Mission Dolores which were purely military and religious establishments. Soon after Richardson received a permit to occupy a specific area where he set up a tent or shack-like structure for his wife, Maria Antonia Martinez and their three children. However, the occupancy of this canvas dwelling supported by wooden poles was of short duration. Thus the embryo of San Francisco was known as *Yerba Buena* although land grants were not issued until September 22, 1835 and then, all house-lots were not to exceed 200 varas square and the same number of varas from the nearby cove. [Report on the condition of the Real Estate within the limits of the City of San Francisco, and the property beyond, within the bounds of the old Mission Dolores, January, 1851.]

After some difficulties due to legal technicalities, Richardson was finally granted 100 varas "in front of the beach in the point of Yerba Buena," providing he serve as official head of the cove to prevent illicit trafficking. Although William A. Richardson constructed the first habitation at *Yerba Buena,* he cannot be regarded as the founder of San Francisco which dates from 1776, upon the founding of the presidio and Mission Dolores. [*Ibid.*] Soon after this agreement, he constructed a wooden dwelling for his family and by the close of 1835, he was acting as harbor master of the cove. This sheltered portion of San Francisco Bay had served as the favorite anchorage of merchants and smugglers since 1824, when the landing place below the San Francisco Presidio was deemed unsafe.

In November 1835, after having served as administrator of Mission Dolores, Jose Joaquin Estudillo applied for 100 varas of land at Yerba Buena, but due to some legal technicalities of the law, was refused. Some time later, his application was referred to the Committee on Municipal Lands which was in favor of granting him a house-lot, but only 100 varas square and not within 200 varas of the beach. [*Ibid.*] In early 1836, shortly after the small group of residents near Mission Dolores had elected Estudillo *Alcalde* of Yerba Buena, he erected a humble dwelling for his wife and their six children who had remained in San Jose. What Dona Estudillo expected has not been established, but it is known that she was not favorably impressed. The only redeeming feature was the wooden flooring, a luxury enjoyed by Californians of that period. Many years later, she spoke of her "first real home", the poorly constructed and most inadequate dwelling of adobe with wooden supports. She dimly recalled her tiny garden of a few clumps of wild iris, lupines and deep blue brodiaea. [Personal interviews with the late Lilly Davis, Elice Cushing and Ynez Estudillo.]

R.H. Dana, Jr., visited the area in December 1836 and later wrote of the newly founded settlement consisting mostly of Yankees. He also observed the harbor where the only vessel at anchor was a Russian brig that had come down to winter and take on a great supply of tallow and grain from "a mission at the head of the bay." [R.H. Dana, Jr., *Two Years Before the Mast,* 1887 Edition, pp. 261, 252.] This establishment was undoubtedly Mission Santa Clara, a flourishing establishment at the height of its prosperity, when it was secularized in December 27, 1836. [Interviews and letters from the Rev. Father Arthur D. Spearman, S.J.] The mission structures stood several miles southeast of its embarcadero at the extreme southern end of the bay.

Great quantities of hides and tallow were also acquired by the equally productive Mission San Jose at the base of the eastern foothills north of Mission Santa Clara. Like the latter mission, its commodities had to be hauled over miles of marshlands to an embarcadero edging the eastern shore of the bay near the present town of Alvarado in Alameda County.

In Yerba Buena, Juana Estudillo and her father, Ygnacio Martinez, had petitioned for four square leagues of his scenic expanse in 1823, but was obliged to wait six years before receiving his provisional grant from Governor Jose Maria de Echeandia. Martinez named it *Nuestra Senora de la Merced,* but by the time he was awarded his formal grant from Governor Juan Bautista in 1842, it had become known as *El Rancho Pinolo.* Pinolo was a palatable food made by the Indians of the area, but in time, the spelling was changed to "pinole." When Dona Estudillo and her children arrived, an immense corral and a large, sprawling adobe dwelling had already been constructed by her father and brothers with the aid of an unknown number of Indians from Mission Dolores. Because Martinez had chosen only skilled and dependable Indians, their quarters were not too distant from the great adobe, beautifully located in a broad, fertile valley about three or four miles southeast of Carquinez Strait, then known as *La Boca del Puerto Dulce.*

Although the ex-neophytes were under constant surveillance, Martinez had a small cannon placed near his home to ward off those who might display too much interest in his many daughters. There were also non-baptized natives in the far mountains, but these were only seen in late fall while gathering relished madrona and toyon berries on the lower slopes. [Interviews with the late Lilly Davis, Elice Cushing and Ynez Estudillo.] According to the late Mrs. Carolyn Hatherly who was born on El Rancho Pinole, the Felipe Briones family received permission to settle on Martinez' acreage in 1831. This may have been because Briones feared the bands of unpredictable natives in the heavily wooded portions of his Rancho *Boca de la Cañada de Pinole,* southeast of Martinez' claim. In 1840, less than a decade later, Felipe was killed by a renegade Indian on Rancho El Pinole and in 1848, Don Ygnacio Martinez died of injuries received during a similar attack, or an encounter with a bear. The great concern, however, were the bands of horse thieves formed by dechristianized mission Indians.

In the late fall of 1836, when Jose Joaquin Estudillo joined his family at El Rancho Pinole, plans to settle his family on acreage south of Luis Maria Peralta's vast holdings were well underway. Because Mission San

Jose was being secularized, Estudillo, who was well acquainted with the ultimate result of secularization, chose a portion of its most northern acreage that for almost forty years served merely as grazing lands. Martinez' offer to assist his son-in-law was most encouraging as was Dona Juana's indomitable courage, profound faith in prayer and belief in the old Spanish proverb: "All is his who has the courage to wish." [*Ibid.*] Estudillo was indeed optimistic, but before long he was to learn that not even a wise man can control his destiny.

2

Grantee of Rancho San Leandro

By mid 1836, while Estudillo was serving as alcalde of Yerba Buena (San Francisco), he had received permission from the Department of California in Monterey to occupy the most northern portion of Mission San Jose's grazing lands. This was known as El Rodeo de Arroyo de San Leandro, named for the ever-flowing stream which marked the northern boundary of the mission's holdings. El Rodeo de Arroyo de San Leandro extended southward from the watercourse to the northern bank of Arroyo de San Lorenzo. San Francisco Bay marked the western boundary. But because the foothills to the east and the land beyond were in excess of the mission's needs, the eastern boundary remained somewhat indefinite. Prior to the establishment of Mission San Jose, this scenic expanse of lowlands and rolling hills was inhabited by countless Costanoan Indians. Their six settlements of various sizes were widely separated but it was not long after the founding of Mission San Jose in 1797 that most of the natives were brought into the association of this establishment.

In late 1836, Estudillo received permission to occupy El Rodeo de Arroyo de San Leandro, but was obliged according to Mexican law to construct a dwelling and improve the land within a year after the permit was granted. On January 8, 1837, he petitioned for four square leagues of the acreage which upon the secularization of Mission San Jose, was deemed public land. Because this amount was far below the quantity within the power of a governor to grant and less than the usual six granted, Estudillo felt confident that his petition would be approved by Juan B. Alvarado, Constitutional Governor of Alta California, and the

Department of California. By this time, he had constructed a simple adobe dwelling about one mile east of San Francisco Bay and near the south bank of Arroyo de San Leandro. Modern maps of San Leandro would place Estudillo's first structure in the vicinity of the Nimitz Freeway overpass at San Leandro Creek. Estudillo later built another adobe dwelling about one mile up the creek. This structure stood a little west of the *Camino Real* as shown on a sketch-map included in Estudillo's *Expediente.* The approximate location of Estudillo's dwelling on this map is marked "Casa de Estudillo." A very small drawing of a simple structure with a definite slanted roof indicates that the dwelling probably had a *topanco* or attic where Estudillo stored his valuable saddles and other items. The flooring of *topanco* in Central California was made of crude, split redwood boards and entered by an outdoor stairway made of the same material. [Transcript of the Proceedings in Case No. 256. Jose Joaquin Estudillo, Claimant, vs. the United States, Defendant for the place named "San Leandro." pp. 7, 11, 12. W.H. Davis, *op. cit.,* p. 539.]

A small portion of land was under cultivation and before long, an unknown number of horses and some three hundred heifers grazed leisurely on the lush lowlands. These were a gift from his father-in-law, Ygnacio Martinez.

In view of the lost petition, Estudillo's deep concern in relation to his rights prompted him to again contact the Department of California. Then, in August 1839, he received a permit to continue his occupancy and development of the acreage. The paper, written by Manuel Jimeno, Secretary to the Governor which states that Estudillo was not to be disturbed in his works or occupancy until the government had determined what was to be done. [Land Case No. 256, p. 85. This document was written by Manuel Jimeno on August 16, 1839.] This was of little comfort to Estudillo who still feared Guillermo Castro would be favored.

In January, 1840, Jose Castro wrote a notice to the Secretary of the Department of California which only added fuel to the glowing embers of controversy between Estudillo and Castro. The translated paper reads in part: "Don Guillermo Castro can establish himself upon the place called "San Leandro" on the part towards the hills without passing beyond the line from north to south formed by the springs on said place, being permitted to make his fields in whatever part of all the land of San Leandro," this concession being understood provisionally until the governor may settle the boundaries which belong to Senor Estudillo, who is actually established on the said site without prejudice to the Indians living therein." (*Ibid,* p. 84.] Governor Alvarado undoubtedly hoped for an early agreement between his nephew and Estudillo. It was his intention to divide the lands of San Leandro equally between the two claimants without regard to the exact quantity, but it was many years before the bitter dispute was finally settled.

In early 1840, great bundles of hides and tallow from Estudillo's herds were being conveyed to his embarcadero at the mouth of San Leandro Creek, which emptied into a slough before reaching the deeper waters of San Francisco Bay. Here, thirty to forty Yankee and South American trading vessels anchored only long enough to take on fresh water, produce and all the hides and tallow their holds could accommodate. Dona Estudillo and her children were now well established in a rambling adobe dwelling near the scenic watercourse. Here on April 15, 1840, she bore the first white child born on Rancho San Leandro. [Mission San Jose Baptismal Records, Vol. II, Entry 7481, June 17, 1840.] On pages 256, 257, and 258 of W.H. Davis' *Sixty Years in California,* we read that Susana Martinez married Captain W.S. Hinckley; after his death, she married William M. Smith who founded the present town of Martinez on the south side of Carquinez Straits in 1848 or 1850.

The translated paper reads in part: "Citizen Jose Joaquin Estudillo, a Mexican by birth, hereby appears before Your Excellency, saying that in order to procure his subsistence and enable himself to support a large family consisting of a wife and ten children, after having served in the army 17 years, four months and some days, on the eighth of January, eighteen hundred and thirty-seven, he petitioned for the tract of land known by the name of Arroyo de San Leandro, containing four square leagues from east to west and having obtained from your Excellency, who extends a generous and protecting patronage towards the inhabitants of this land, permission to settle himself and continue his labors, meanwhile the proper legal proceedings there upon should be concluded which he has accordingly done.

"Your Excellency, during the space of five years, five months and some days, and his petition having been mislaid in the office of the Secretary of State, he renews his application only accompanying the assembled plat of the aforesaid land in order that in consideration thereof, you may determine what you may esteem proper. Therefore, he prays, Your Excellency, in the exercise of your goodness, to consider his petition favorably by which he will receive the kindness which he asks and expects, rendering with Your Excellency his everlasting gratitude." [Land Case No. 256, pp. 48, 49.]

On October 16, 1842, Governor Juan B. Alvarado granted Estudillo a portion of a Rancho San Leandro. The translated document reads in part: "I declare Don Joaquin Estudillo to be the owner in property of a part of the tract of land known by the name of "San Leandro," bounded on the north by the Arroyo of San Leandro, on the east by the places where the waters from the springs [derramaderos] on the lands which the Indians who are now established there occupy, waste themselves, thence on the south side in a straight line to the Arroyo of San Lorenzo, and without embracing the land which said Indians cultivate, and on the west by the sea." [Land Case No. 256, pp. 48-52.]

The tract allotted to Estudillo embraced one league (4,438 acres), more or less, as was shown on a sketch map accompanying Estudillo's Expediente. He was to understand that the remaining surplus was to be part of the Nation and if he did not conform to these conditions, he would automatically forfeit his right to the land and it would be granted to another. "Therefore, I order that this title being held as firm and valid, an entry be made thereof in the respective book [of registry] and that this be delivered to the interested party for his security and other ends. Given at Monterey on the sixteenth day of August, one thousand, eight hundred and forty-two." [*Ibid.*] This document was written by Manuel Jimeno, Secretary to Governor Alvarado and the accompanying sketch map was drawn by order of the Prefect.

Eighteen hundred and forty-four marked the eve of California's turbulent and political existence and the birth of the Estudillos' last child, Jesus Maria, the diarist of *Journal for 1862*.

By 1844, Dona Estudillo and her daughters were obliged to curb their extravagances especially in the acquisition of expensive fabrics, elegant laces, fans, slippers and other luxuries from trading vessels anchored in San Francisco Bay. They had been accustomed to board vessels upon invitation of the trader and browse about while he and Estudillo leisurely sipped choice brandy in his private headquarters. For the past two years, Estudillo's vaqueros had reported a gradual disappearance of horses used to round up cattle for slaughter. Despite arming his most competent vaqueros, the problem became worse and ultimately placed Estudillo in embarrassing financial circumstances. Personal explanation for his indebtedness to merchants and traders was not always possible.

On October 11, 1845, Joaquin Estudillo wrote to one of his creditors begging to be excused for his indebtedness. This letter was addressed to Cesario Lataillade of Santa Barbara who was a member of a Mexican trading firm, although of French descent. The translated message reads in part: "My friend, everybody, or let's say the people hereabouts, at the present time, know how to take as many horses from me as I have, and so I can't slaughter cattle to comply with my creditors as I wish I could; for in spite of having taken due care of the herd, I gained nothing. . . ." [Photostat of original letter, courtesy of Rev. Brother Veronius Henry, F.S.O., Archivist of Mont La Salle, Napa, California.]

Estudillo added that matters were in such a bad state that he could hardly kill fifty cattle for their hides and tallow. "So my friend, patience until next year which will be one of the best." [*Ibid.*]

W.H. Davis wrote: "Merchants and traders sold to the rancheros and Californios whatever they wanted to any reasonable amount and gave them credit from one slaughter to another." R.H. Dana wrote: the fondness for the dress among the women is excessive. He noted the women who had boarded the brig, *Pilgrim,* while it anchored in the harbor of Monterey. "They used to spend whole days aboard our vessel examining fine clothes and ornaments and frequently made purchases at a rate which would have made a seamstress or waiting maid in Boston open her eyes." [R.H. Dana, *op. cit.,* 1887 edition, p. 87.]

While this practice was of some comfort to the honorable Estudillo, it did not solve his problem. His troubles were not unique, nor did the following year, which was to be "one of the best" improve his financial status. With Spanish pride, the family failed to accept financial reverses, and to all outward appearances reveled in good fortune by their extravagant way of life. In some cases, traders and merchants deliberately encouraged extended credit to Californios who lived and entertained lavishly despite their obligations knowing that in time, they would be obliged to forfeit sections of their land in exchange for their indebtedness. This was especially practiced after the close of the war with Mexico.

In early 1848, word arrived that gold had been discovered on the American river; this again upset the balance of affairs in California and although the news created startling changes in the behavior of many, it failed to arouse Joaquin Estudillo. He and many others knew of a similar event that took place in 1842 in the foothills of the San Fernando Valley, and that the excitement dissipated almost as rapidly as it began. Of greater interest to Estudillo and his many relatives in southern California, was the signing of the Treaty of Peace on February 2, and ratified by the United States on March 10, 1848.

Affairs in California had been in a state of turmoil for over a decade owing to political upheavals in Mexico. This of course created unrest and confusion in the Department of California at Monterey, but had little or no direct effect upon the Spanish and Mexican rancheros; however, they feared that their sons might be forced to serve Mexico during its various trials. B.I. Hayes, who was well acquainted with many of the Californios, wrote that the acquisition of California by the United States produced little change in the habits of these people. [B.I. Hayes, *Notes on California Affairs,* (loose papers).]

Reverend Walter Colton wrote: "The Californios as a community never had any profound reverence for their nominal flag. They regarded it only as evidence of their colonial relations to Mexico; a relations for which they felt neither affection nor pride." [Rev. Walter Colton, *op. cit.,* pp. 435, 436.] Colton's opinion was not shared by Governor Juan Bautista Alvarado who maintained that the Californios' allegiance to Mexico remained strong even after the Stars and Stripes displaced the Mexican colors. Colton added that Mariano Guadalupe Vallejo, the most influential man among the Californios, always evinced a repugnance to Mexican rule. [*Ibid.*] Whether this applied to Estudillo has not been ascertained, however, he must have given a sigh of relief upon the close of the conflict.

Now that Rancho San Leandro lay under the Stars and Stripes, Joaquin Estudillo hoped that horse and cattle thieves would be exterminated or at least lessened under American law. This was wishful thinking. However, he and other ranchers were compensated in part by the demand for agricultural products. Beans, onions, squash, corn and potatoes were the main vegetables demanded by the increasing number of trading vessels. San Francisco and the mining communities paid well for beef and grain. Cattle sold from fifty to seventy-five dollars per head in Stockton, the main center of distribution to the mining area of present Stanislaus, Tuolumne and Mariposa Counties. Hides were now being made into saddles, reins, buckets, miners' boots and other useful items. However, this period of good fortune was not of long duration. Less than two years after the discovery of gold, strife struck again with the influx of squatters. Law suits were common. During the ensuing years, California's grantees were obliged to spend fortunes in legal representation to have their acreage confirmed and patented by the U.S. Government. This and the great drought of 1863 and 1864, when lean, thirsty cattle brought only one-tenth of their value, ultimately closed the era of the Dons, their magnificent haciendas and the most colorful period in the history of California.

3

The Decline of Rancho San Leandro

It has not been ascertained when the first squatter fastened himself upon Rancho San Leandro, but by 1845 a Bruno Valencia had already cultivated an area edging the north bank of San Lorenzo Creek, the southern boundary of Estudillo's grant. [Land Case No. 256, p. 554.] In September of the following year (1846), Thomas Eagar, then a boy of sixteen, chanced upon the rancho while exploring the eastern shore of San Francisco Bay. He met Estudillo in the vicinity of his home and although the family had guests at the time, Eagar was invited to join the group and remain for a few days if he wished. During the boy's stay, a friendship formed that was to last for many years, but before long, Jose Joaquin Estudillo was forced to question other strangers, who, unlike Eagar, merely chanced upon his acreage.

Spring of 1849 marked the beginning of the great stampede to California. Most of the newcomers made their way directly to the gold-bearing regions. However, not all were in search of the precious metal and some changed their objective upon arrival. The incoming tide deposited many noble persons to California's soil, but it also washed in the dregs of society. Some were the dyed-in-the-wool scoundrels with a total disregard of rights and of the misfortunes of their fellowmen. Although plans differed, their common objective was to acquire acreage and wealth with far less effort than by pick and shovel labor. Now that California no longer lay under Mexican rule, some concluded that the Spanish and Mexican Californios had lost their rights and that their fertile lands could be had by merely setting up a claim and an unsightly shelter wherever they chose. Several had learned that if they encoun-

19

tered trouble over their claims, there were rancheros who would not be able to point out the boundaries of their holdings unless it was a body of water, a stream, a ridge, or some obvious formation.

There were also immigrants who came with farming equipment knowing that they could not be legally evicted from their chosen sites until definite boundaries had been established upon the confirmation of land grants by the United States Government. Instead of confirming all land grants and settling the matter of legal ownership upon the close of the war with Mexico, it was not until 1851 that the United States Government formed the Board of Land Commissioners to solve the problems of those who had acquired acreage prior to 1846.

The decline of Rancho San Leandro stems mainly from the land problem. However, other complex factors contributed to its collapse. Leonard Pitt's book, *The Decline of the Californios* best presents the injustices and problems thrust upon the Spanish and Mexican grantees prior to and after 1851, when the United States Board of Land Commissioners was established.

By the fall of 1849, while great pumpkins, squashes, peppers, red beans and onions continued to ripen on the still-warm earth, ominous clouds began to cast shadows of trouble over Rancho San Leandro with the appearance of more squatters. One of the first to become entangled over land rights was Thomas W. Mulford and a few of his companions. After rowing across San Francisco Bay and finding a suitable landing-place on the eastern shore, the strangers disembarked to study the area before continuing their plans. They finally chose an area a few miles south of Estudillo's home and a little east of the marshlands edging the bay. At that time, Mr. John B. Ward, an Irishman by birth, was managing Rancho San Leandro for Jose Joaquin Estudillo who had found American customs and laws too perplexing and complicated.

Mr. Ward was the first to find the crude shelter of the squatters, but because it appeared to be merely a duck-hunters' camp, it caused little concern. Before long, however, improvements were noted that indicated plans for permanent residence, whereupon Mr. Ward decided to question their motives. Although Mulford was only about twenty years of age, he spoke for the group and made it very clear that he and his friends resented interference and intended to remain. After repeated visits, Mr. Ward finally convinced Estudillo that the ugly situation might be solved by simply relinquishing a small portion of the rancho to the Yankee intruders. This was done, but sometime later, boundary disputes arose as the squatters demanded more land and rights. Unpleasantries continued during the ensuing years until 1867, when troubles between Mulford and the Estudillos were finally settled by a court decision in favor of the Estudillo family.

On April 8, 1852, bedridden Jose Joaquin Estudillo dictated his will in the presence of his friend, Juan B. Alvarado and the Estudillos' attorneys, Messrs. John S. Saunders, William W. Smith and W.R. Benjamin. By that time, the U.S. Board of Land Commissioners had opened offices in San Francisco, and because Estudillo was obliged to place his claim for Rancho San Leandro before these gentlemen, Estudillo revised the will he had dictated in April of the previous year, which was witnessed only by Alvarado and members of the family. [Land Case No. 256, pp. 67, 78, 79.]

The translated document states in part that Estudillo owned the home in which he and his wife were living and seven frame houses situated at various points near his embarcadero. One-half of the rancho was to be left to his widow in addition to one-half of the two or three thousand head of cattle, and half or more than that number of sheep and fifty horses of all classes. The other half of the rancho was to be divided equally among his children. Juana Estudillo was to have their home and all furnishings. Estudillo had settled accounts with a few merchants, but by casualty, any debts against the estate were to be paid by his son, Jose Ramon, whom he appointed executor of the estate. [*Ibid.*] Estudillo's indebtedness to his friend, Guillermo (William) Hartnell was to receive immediate attention and ". . . whenever my son-in-law, Guillermo Davis (William Heath) demands two hundred head of cattle or five thousand dollars in silver which I owe him, be punctually paid to the satisfaction of all parties as they may agree which sum with preference shall be taken from the common mass of property previous to the division of my estate." [*Ibid.*]

Of Estudillo's nine children, only Jose Ramon received special mention in his father's will. In addition to a portion of the rancho, he was to receive forty head of cattle ". . . to be selected to his satisfaction of the kind and quality which he shall be pleased to take in consideration of my said sons, having been the one who, with assiduous toil and good behavior, labored in the foundation of the rancho and the augmentation of the herds." [*Ibid.*] Estudillo recommended that the executors of his will ". . . arrange without delay or respect that which I should make with my attorneys charged with the negotiating of the proper confirmation thereof before the United States Commissioners, and that they pay all the necessary expenses of surveyors and all thus which may be necessary to obtain the secure and legal possession of the said property." [*Ibid.*]

On May 31, 1852, Jose Joaquin Estudillo's claim for the place known as San Leandro was filed in the offices of George Fisher, Secretary of the U.S. Board of Land Commissioners in San Francisco.

Don Jose Joaquin Estudillo's claim for the land known as *San Leandro* reads as follows on pages 48 through 52 in the proceedings of Land Case No. 256.

"Petitioner, a Mexican by birth, respectfully represents that on the 8th day of January 1837, for the benefit of himself and family, he petitioned the Constitutional Governor of the Department of California according to law, for a grant of the tract of land situated in said Department and known as the Arroyo de San Leandro which said petition was lost or mislaid in the Office of the Government Secretary. That in consequence of said loss, your petitioner afterwards, on the 28th day of June 1842, renewed his said petition according to law for said grant of said loss to the Governor as foresaid of said Department and at that time, Juan B. Alvarado, on the 16th day of October 1842, received a grant of a part of said tract of land made according to law by said Governor which said part is described in said grant as follows.

"A part of the tract of land known by the name of San Leandro, bounded northerly with the creek of San Leandro, easterly with the spillings from the springs on the lands occupied by Indians that at the present time are established there. From this point, running in a straight line on the south boundary up to the creek of San Leandro, and we think embracing the lands cultivated by said Indians and westerly with the sea, containing one league (the setio de ganada) more or less. That the said portions of said land contained within said boundaries and actually occupied and cultivated by said Indians was very inconsiderable, not excluding three acres and that said Indians have long since abandoned the same, and now occupy, with the consent of petitioner, another portion of the land granted as aforesaid to petitioner.

"Petitioner further represents that he has carried out and performed the terms and conditions of said grant and has complied with the terms in relation to said grant. That in consequence of the loss of his first mentioned petition, he received an official permit to settle and occupy said land on the 16th day of August 1839 and has occupied and possessed the same ever since as the lawful owner thereof. (Signed) Saunders, Hepburn and Baluy, for Petitioner."

Several papers from Estudillo's Expediente had already been presented to Samuel D. King, Surveyor for the Department of California; then in charge of the archives of the former Spanish and Mexican Territory of Alta California.

On June 1, 1852, Juana Estudillo invited a priest to reside with the family to administer the last Sacraments of the Catholic Church before her husband's departure from this earth. A day or two later, as his condition worsened, he was taken to a San Francisco hospital where he died on June 7, in the presence of his beloved wife and the priest who had also remained by his bedside all through the night. Countless numbers attended his services on the following day in the chapel of Mission Dolores where, in 1823, he had claimed Juana Maria del Carmen Martinez as his bride. Of added grief to the family was that they were unable to abide by Estudillo's last wish: ". . . when I shall have deceased, I commend that my body be interred in the habit of our Father Saint Francis at the door of the Church of Mission San Jose."

In J.M. Estudillo's *Journal for 1867,* he wrote that his father died on June 7, 1852. Burial Record No. 5724 at Mission Dolores that Don Jose Joaquin Estudillo was born at "Monte Rey" and he was fifty-two years of age when he died. The service was conducted by Fr. Flavien Fontain on June 8, 1852. By request, Dona Juana Estudillo's father, Ygnacio Martinez, was buried at Mission San Jose on June 24, 1848, several days after he had died of wounds inflicted by a bear on El Rancho Pinole. The reason Don Jose Joaquin Estudillo was not buried at Mission San Jose may have been because at that time it lacked a resident priest. [Land Case 256, pp. 76-79.] Heavily veiled women and the men with bowed heads wept unabashed as the mortal remains of Don Estudillo were lowered into the hallowed ground near the graves of his son, Jose Maria and his daughter, Maria Filomena de Guadalupe.

Miss Ynez Estudillo said that Jesus Maria Estudillo searched for his father's grave in the mid 1870s, in vain, because by late 1853, the outskirts of the cemetery at Mission Dolores where his father was buried had no longer any markers. The only recognizable graveyard was the small area adjacent to the chapel which dates from 1781. Here among many handsome monuments, J.M. paused to study the marker on the grave of his father's esteemed friend, Don Luis Antonio Arguello who was born at the San Francisco Presidio in 1794 and died on March 28, 1830.

From the beginning of 1850 to June 1854, 300 interments were made in the Mission Dolores Cemetery and 4,450 at the Yerba Buena Cemetery, established in February 1850, as a public burial ground between the mission and the settlement of Yerba Buena. [Frank Soule, *op. cit.*, pp. 593-596.] San Francisco's Lone Mountain cemetery was inaugurated on May 30, 1854.

After her husband's death, necessity rather than preference forced Juana Estudillo to acquaint herself with the history and laws of this country. Because she had not mastered the English language, she purchased *Compendio de la Historia de los Estados o Republica de America* which had recently been published in New York. This book was published by A.S. Barnes and Company of New York in 1852.

Now that more squatters, litigations and indebtedness were curbing her freedom to indulge in luxuries and social extravagances, she determined to exercise more control in sales and rentals of her properties. Davis had long noted his mother-in-law's business ability but was somewhat shocked when she became so ambitious and shrewd in her policies that it became quite the subject of conversation in the small community of San Leandro. Most amazing was that she demanded and received higher rentals than her neighbors, the Peraltas, whose acreage and structures were equally desirable. In 1858, an article appears in San Leandro's *Gazette* complaining strongly of the high prices charged by owners of land to tenants. This was aimed mainly at the management of the Estudillo *rancho*. [Personal interviews with the late Ferdinand Eber of San Leandro.] Occasionally, J.M. accompanied his mother to El Rancho Pinole to visit her mother who had been a widow since 1848, and to contact the manager of Juana's inherited portion of the rancho. The journey was lengthy and often trying, yet the beauty of the country compensated for the dust from spinning carriage wheels. Most of the stretch was one vast field of grain without fences except for those that kept cattle up in the rolling pasture lands. [J.W. Harlan, *op. cit.*, p. 169.]

4

Shifting Patterns

Alameda County was formed on March 25, 1853 [William Halley, *The Centennial Year Book of Alameda County, California*, p. 71], but this and politics did not particularly interest Juana Estudillo until June of the same year when the county government began to function in the nearby town of Alvarado, the designated county seat. During the Mission Period, Mission San Jose maintained an embarcadero on the southeastern shore of San Francisco Bay. After secularization, a community was established in the vicinity of the landing-place which later became known as *New Haven* and then *Alvarado*. By 1853, this settlement had about 300 inhabitants, one or two modest inns and a stage station.

Fearing that the development of this small community would decrease the value of her and her children's properties, she determined that nothing was to interrupt their income and unrestrained way of life. Messrs. Ward and Davis, co-managers of Rancho San Leandro were surprised to contact county politicians who probably could be influenced to change the location of the county seat. Such a long journey was indeed needless. Furthermore, the upper story of a store utilized for county affairs was deemed neither desirable nor a safe place for county offices.

Ward and Davis' efforts had barely begun when several politicians began to grumble on their own volition. Those who lived in Oakland found the twenty-mile stage journey to Alvarado time consuming, unbearably hot and dusty. Reliable stage service could not be expected during the rainy season. To be bogged down on the lowlands during the torrential rain was unthinkable. Another objection was that Alvarado was only twelve miles from the Santa Clara county line.

By fall of 1854, plans for relocating the county seat to San Leandro were well underway. In December of that year (1854), the Estudillo family donated to the County of Alameda a block of land for a proposed courthouse. However, the deed stipulated it would remain county property only as long as the county seat remained in San Leandro. In the event of a change, the land was to be returned to the family.

W.H. Davis, in his *Sixty Years in California,* wrote that in June, 1855, after the Board of Supervisors for the County of Alameda had voted in favor of San Leandro as the county seat, a sudden fire destroyed Juana Estudillo's home in which the meeting had taken place. Davis was inclined to believe that it had probably been set by one or more persons who were determined that the county seat remain in Alvarado. [W.H. Davis, *Sixty Years in California,* p. 545.] Since Davis did not write of repairs or construction of another dwelling, some readers are apt to conclude that the burned structure was their adobe home near San Leandro Creek, but this had already been in ruins by 1853. It has not been definitely established when the Estudillos occupied their spacious, frame home, but Davis wrote that in 1850, when Juana Estudillo's mother visited the family, she viewed Rancho San Leandro from the cupola of her daughter's home [*Ibid.*] This ornamental structure topped the second story of the fourteen-room, frame dwelling and was the only portion destroyed by the fire. Because the second story was subsequently finished off as a flat-topped structure, it lost the distinctive charm which had prompted the small community of San Leandro to name it the *Estudillo Mansion.* It was indeed San Leandro's largest and most imposing dwelling. However, the word mansion would not conform with present-day standards. The Estudillo mansion stood on the northwest corner of present West Estudillo Avenue and Carpentier Street, named in honor of Horace W. Carpentier who had assisted in the forming of Alameda County and later served as Mayor of Oakland. On June 7, 1964, a bronze marker was placed on the site under the auspices of the California State Park Commission and St. Leander's Parish. It reads: "California Registered Historical Landmark No. 279."

Despite controversies created by the fire, the county seat remained in San Leandro until, due to some technicality of the law, Alvarado succeeded in retrieving county records. Once again, this settlement served as the county seat, but only for a few weeks. Finally, on February 8,

1856, after countless political wranglings, San Leandro was formally designated as the seat of Alameda County by the state Legislature. A little more than five months later, county affairs began to function in a temporary structure until 1857, upon the completion of a permanent courthouse on the block of land previously donated to the county by the Estudillo family. The Alameda County Courthouse in San Leandro was occupied in February 1857, but was damaged beyond repair during a severe earthquake in 1868. In 1873, when the county seat was transferred to Oakland, J.M. Estudillo, a staunch Democrat, was nominated County Clerk. The land occupied by the former courthouse then reverted to the Estudillo family who later donated it to the Catholic Church.

In January 1856 the Estudillos believed that their troubles with Guillermo Castro were terminated when a written agreement was reached in relation to the eastern boundary of Rancho San Leandro. [Land Case No. 256, pp. 562, 567, 599. This agreement was written and sealed by L.W. Sloat, Notary Public.] However, some months later, another misunderstanding arose and after nine months of renewed tension and further surveys, a new agreement was formed and signed by Castro and the Estudillos including Maria Dolores and Jesus Maria, who, being less than eighteen years of age, were under the guardianship of Juana Estudillo.

The dividing line between Rancho San Leandro and Guillermo Castro's claim was to extend ". . . from the northerly foundation of an adobe formerly occupied by Indian Sylvester, now deceased, thence in a straight line northwesterly passing through the center of the lagoon or small lake between the hills to San Leandro Creek." [Land Case No. 256, p. 563.]

By that time, Sylvester's brother, Annisitto, had also died and squatters had driven his younger brothers and their families from the areas the neophytes had occupied for more than twenty years. This injustice and total disregard for their welfare was frowned upon by Guillermo Castro who employed two of Sylvester's sons and their families as household servants, vaqueros and tenders of his vast agricultural areas. Sylvester's younger brothers, who had fled to the lagoon, were similarly employed by the Estudillos. A few were ultimately housed within the base of a large windmill to the rear of the Estudillo mansion. One or more of the Estudillos' vaqueros and their families chose to remain in the vicinity of the lagoon despite the prevalence of stalking cougars and huge, lumbering bears.

By 1856, San Francisco merchants were demanding more for cattle, sheep, hay and agricultural products. To further their income, the Estudillo family constructed a two-story hotel at the convergence of the two main routes connecting Oakland with Santa Clara County and a little south of the covered bridge that spanned San Leandro Creek. Named the "Estudillo House," the well-appointed hostelry was soon filled with guests and became the locale of innumerable social functions, especially during the 1860s.

One of the most notable gatherings at the *Estudillo House* took place on December 22, 1858, the annual Christmas Festival of the San Leandro's Bachelors' Club. The main attraction of the evening was Lotta Crabtree (Charlotte Mignon), then but eleven years of age and known for her excellent dancing, modesty and charming manners. [J.W. Harlan, *op. cit.*, pp. 136, 137.]

Juana Estudillo frequently attended social gatherings at the hotel and invariably wore a gold broach with a portrait of her late husband. During the Victorian Period, these broaches, which could also be worn as lockets, were known as *Mourning Broaches*.

The Estudillo House stood on the southwest corner of present Davis Street and Washington Avenue previously known as the *Alvarado Road* and later named *Watkins Street* in honor of Joseph S. Watkins, an early Assemblyman of Alameda County. In the 1880s, it was not uncommon for 500 or more guests to enjoy the plush parlors, rear garden, recreational area and especially the magnificent grape arbor. The vines, cuttings from the Peraltas' vineyards, ultimately shaded an area of forty by one-hundred feet in dimension. During this period and in the early 1900s, the Estudillo House had twenty two rooms, a large dining room, lounge, a billiard room and several small card rooms. Among its distinguished guests were James Fair, former Governor James Budd, James Duval Phelan and the Ghirardellis of San Francisco. In the *C.A.C.C. Touring Guide and Road Book, 1898,* we read that the rate was $1.50 a day per person; excellent meals could be had for forty cents. The historic structure was razed in 1929 to accommodate new buildings and the widening of Davis Street.

Despite its popularity, the family was ultimately forced to sell the establishment, its adjacent saloon and its extensive recreational areas.

J.M. had been tutored since he was about six or seven years of age and because he was often in the presence of Messrs. Ward and Davis, he spoke English fluently, but never in the presence of his mother. In the spring of 1856, a priest from an eastern college visited the Estudillos to recommend sending the boy to the institution he represented. J.M., he said, would readily make friends among its many American students, but if at first he felt lonesome or displaced, he could find companions among boys from Southern California who were also descendants of early Spanish families. Juana Estudillo was assured that J.M. would receive a thorough education, spiritual guidance and special care in the event of illness. Ward and Davis were wholeheartedly in favor of the suggestion mainly because they felt J.M. would benefit by being with students of varied backgrounds and ancestry. Juana Estudillo, however, dismissed the subject without her approval mainly because she could not bear the thought of having her youngest child so far from home. [Personal interviews with Ynez Estudillo.] Juana had long known of nearby Santa Clara College and its preparatory department and that boarding-students were permitted to spend vacations at home if their parents or wards gave timely notice, settled all accounts and forwarded money to defray traveling expenses. J.M.'s homeward journey would be merely a short horse-drawn omnibus ride to San Jose where he could board a stage, and under favorable weather conditions, be in San Leandro within five or six hours. Furthermore his mother also welcomed the idea that she would be able to visit him on Sundays and during the Easter season which she usually spent with her esteemed friend, Maria de la Soledad Ortega de Arguello, who lived but a short distance from the college and adjacent Mission Church. [Personal interviews with the Rev. Father Arthur D. Spearman, S.J.]

Toward the close of the spring semester in 1856, J.M. and his mother visited the President of Santa Clara College to arrange for his admission as a boarding student in its preparatory department. Before admittance, all prospective students were closely screened by the president. Regardless of age, they were required to abide by the exacting rules of the Jesuit institution and of the Roman Catholic Faith, the unrevokable obligations of the church. Non-Catholics were not excluded from admission if they pledged not to discuss religion with other students. They were welcome to attend church services, but students of the Catholic Faith were expected to attend all Sacraments, early morning and evening rosary and Sunday services. All students, regardless of age, rose at six o'clock and retired by eight P.M. Only the advanced were permitted in the study hall until nine-thirty P.M., when a light meal was served as a reward for their diligence. Unless a boy was ill, he was to be at meals promptly and properly attired including well-polished boots. Santa Clara College maintained an excellent library and scientific equipment, but did not furnish pens, ink, paper and other classroom necessities. These could be purchased in San Jose upon permission to leave the campus for that purpose. [*Ibid.*]

September 1856, found the sensitive and retiring boy at Santa Clara College trying to adjust himself to a new way of life. Because he was deeply religious and accustomed to obeying his mother and elder members of the family, Juana Estudillo was confident that he would abide by the rigid schedule and rules of the institution. The financial obligation was, however, of deep concern since tuition fees were to be paid in full on or before the beginning of each semester. Attorney fees for surveys mounted with the continuance of Land Case No. 256. More and more squatters filed suit against the family, which in some cases resulted in favor of the new-comers. An example of this took place about a month before the death of Jose Joaquin Estudillo in 1852, when Franklin Wray presented his problem before the Justice of the Peace. He said: "After I settled on the land and got my house built, I had trouble with them. Davis and the Estudillos and others with them tore down my house, so we had a law suit about it. After that, I rebuilt my house and that was torn down. I do not know by whom, but it was supposed to be by the same parties." [Land Case No. 256, pp. 23, 24, 57.] Proof was established that Wray had constructed his dwelling without consent from Estudillo, but because Messrs. Ward and Davis had not received permission from their father-in-law to demolish Wray's structure, Justice of the Peace, Edson Adams, ordered the Estudillos to pay Wray for the damage and court expenses. [*Ibid.*]

On May 7, 1857, Judge Ogden Hoffman of the U.S. District Court, ". . . adjudged and decreed that the claim of the Board of Commissioners is a good and valid claim and the same is hereby confirmed." [*Ibid.*, p. 734.] It was adjudged that Rancho San Leandro was ". . . bounded on the north by the Arroyo de San Leandro; on the west by San Francisco Bay (El Mar); on the east by a line drawn from San Leandro Creek through the places where the waters from the springs on the lands which the Indians established there in 1842, washed themselves (Derramederos); and on the south by a straight line from the termination of the line last mentioned at the waters of said springs drawn to the Arroyo de San Lorenzo in such a manner as to touch and exclude the lands which the said Indians had cultivated; and thence by said arroyo to the bay being the same land granted to said Estudillo." [*Ibid.*] Mr. Campbell, counsel for the Estudillos then asked for an amended decree which would more clearly express the intention and meaning of the original decree. There being no opposition from the District Court, the amended decree was granted.

John B. Ward continued to manage the affairs of the rancho, attended to J.M.'s tuition at Santa Clara College and occasionally sent him small amounts of money for supplies, candy, stage and omnibus-fares and other expenses. The boy was well aware of his mother's financial difficulties. Under "Expenditures" in his *Journal for 1861* he wrote: "For the College, $309.25 in several different sums to the amount of $45.00." Because periodic payments wre usually not approved by the college, it is quite likely that Mr. Ward had previously presented Juana Estudillo's problems before the Jesuits who then made an exception to the rule. Another notation in the same journal attesting J.M.'s concern reads: "Before beads (evening rosary) I felt a little homesick of some way and thought of the great debts that we have at present. I console myself only by thinking what God may please to do." When J.M. could no longer concentrate upon his studies because payments due the college were long over-due, he requested permission to contact the San Jose Express Office and inquire for mail addressed to the institution. If none had arrived and the Oakland stage was due, he waited and prayed he would not be obliged to report the futility of his journey to the president. Letters from home rarely eased his troubled mind, least of all, those from his mother. In his *Journal for 1861* he wrote: "Received a letter from my mother, not very good news. Davis has put a suit against the family."

In 1862, after countless surveys, several of which were thought to be erroneous, the United States District Court contended that only one league could be legally confirmed and that the exact boundaries of the Estudillos' claim could only be derived after the limits of Castro's grant had been determined. It appeared to the court that one square league more or less comprised 7010 or 8070 acres according to the agreement between the Estudillos and Guillermo Castro.

On July 15, 1863, the United States Supreme Court finally confirmed Rancho San Leandro, and on the same day, a patent for 6,829.58 acres was issued by the United States Government. This, however, was not the termination of the Estudillos' difficulties. Squatter problems continued. J.M. had long been aware of the family's problems, but his concern deepened after he left Santa Clara College in June 1864. Because he had studied bookkeeping and was exceedingly neat and methodical, Mr. Ward placed him in charge of records pertaining to sales, rentals, leases and various other business transactions. Juana Estudillo disapproved of Mr. Ward's plans for the boy's future. They pleaded with J.M. to return to college and study for a degree, but he did not return, mainly because his mother and sister insisted he study law. Mr. Nugent, however, felt that by working for Mr. Ward for awhile at least, he would be prepared to enter the mercantile field.

On July 6, 1864, J.M. wrote: "I heard from Mr. Ward that he had sold a part of my spot of land, a hundred acres, I believe for twelve thousand dollars. I am sorry that this particular spot should have been sold. I believe this to be the finest piece on the Rancho, below the town and all along the creek."

In 1861, an Act was passed by the Probate Court and Court of Sessions in and for the County of Alameda "authorizing Juana M. Estudillo to sell and convey the interest in certain real estate for her infant child, Jesus Maria Estudillo." [W. Halley, *op. cit.,* p. 159.] Many years later, J.M. said he was induced to "sign some papers before he became of age, whereby he lost his rightful inherited portion of Rancho San Leandro." [Personal interview with the late Mr. Ferdinand Eber of San Leandro.]

On August 16, 1864, he added: "The family owes now, one hundred and seven thousand dollars at interest. The greatest sum is due the Hibernia Society (in San Francisco). Of San Leandro, there are at present unsold, two thousand, four hundred acres now selling for one hundred dollars per acre. The two ranchos below of forty thousand acres will no doubt be sold at a loss of ten to fifteen thousand dollars. San Leandro is all to be sold. Mr. Ward takes upon himself the whole of the family debt, giving my mother eighty thousand dollars, twenty-five thousand to each of the younger children, that is Magdalena and myself. Lola's property will be separated very soon. If the value of property increases, as I have good reason to think, Mr. Ward will come out a winner; but it appears to me that he takes upon himself too much responsibility. He has to pay my mother interest on this eighty thousand dollars."

J.M. had good reason to believe that the family's holdings would increase in value as did Mr. Ward, who was well aware of the prices properties in Oakland had brought during the previous year. Improved lands in orchards or agricultural products readily commanded $1000 per acre that a few years prior to 1864, sold for $100. Other matters of equal concern were also brought to the attention of the young bookkeeper. On September 12, 1867, he wrote: "Jose Antonio and Vicente (his brothers) were with me in the office some time during the day, seeing their accounts. Jose Antonio was very much surprised to see that his interest had been sold to Mr. Ward by my mother when she sold him interest in the ranch. Jose Antonio had signed a deed to my mother conveying his interest for safe-keeping at the time he left for Washoe (in 1861 or 1862). Now it will be investigated and see how it happened that such a transaction took place." [J.M. Estudillo, *Journal for 1864.*]

1864 marked J.M.'s first year as a bookkeeper and was the second year of California's tragic drought. By December 1863, the Estudillos' friends and relatives in Southern California had already lost thousands of cattle, sheep and horses for want of water and pasturage. Don Abel Stearns lost about 7000 head of cattle and thousands more were butchered merely for their hides and tallow. Cattle on Rancho San Leandro suffered less severely, but conditions worsened with the beginning of 1864. From January through most of March, not one drop of moisture fell upon the parched land. Each day, the Estudillos prayed for rain. A few showers fell in late March, but not enough to benefit their crops or grazing areas. Then in late May, heavy rains did more damage than good. [*Ibid.*]

On July 29, 1864, J.M. attended the last Mass conducted by the Rev. Father Callen in a hall of San Leandro's Beatty Hotel. Then on the following Sunday, August 7, he awakened early to pick flowers from his mother's garden which he carefully arranged on the altar of San Leandro's first Catholic Church. It was to be dedicated that morning by the Most Reverend Archbishop Joseph Sadoc Alemany. Before noon, the handsome edifice was blessed and named "Saint Leander's Church." According to J.M.'s journal of that year, it "was crowded to suffocation." The dedication ceremonies were followed by Mass conducted by Rector-Father James Callan and two sermons delivered by Archbishop Alemany; one in English, the other in Spanish. Alemany called the new edifice "the little gem," yet it was the largest and most imposing church in Alameda County.

The bell in the steeple of St. Leander's Church was a gift from Mrs. Ygnacio Peralta. It was said to have been imported from Spain in 1846 by Vicente Peralta to serve at his private oratory or chapel near his home in present Oakland's Temescal district. About 1912, the steeple bell was replaced by a larger one cast in the United States. The Peralta bell weighs about 100 pounds and presently hangs in a wooden tower to the rear of St. Leander's School, first known as St. Mary's School, located near the northeast corner of Clarke Street and West Estudillo Avenue. In 1956, the writer was permitted to climb the tower in order to find the date of casting on the bell. However, the only discernible inscription reads: "Deyres Bordeaux" under a small symbol resembling a Greek cross.

The first public religious service held in San Leandro was conducted in 1853 by Methodists in an oak grove in the vicinity of present San Leandro's community Library Center on Estudillo Avenue. The community's first house of worship was the First Methodist Church built in 1856 on land donated by the Estudillos, who also donated property to the Presbyterians.

That evening, all members of the Estudillo family gathered in the mansion to enjoy a beautiful dinner in honor of the Archbishop. Although the relationship between William Heath Davis and his brother-in-law, John B. Ward had eased, their differences were not forgotten. Davis and several of his children attended the gathering, but Mrs. Davis, who was again heavy with child, had begged to be excused.

Seven days later, J.M. wrote: ". . . Lola (his sister, Maria Dolores) took communion at eleven o'clock. The pews were sold at auction and Mr. Ward bid for the two front rows and as no one was there to offer a higher bid he got them." [J.M. Estudillo's *Journal for 1864*.] That afternoon, Lola was married to Mr. Charles H. Cushing, the first wedding to take place in St. Leander's Church. By that time about six or seven thousand acres of Juana Estudillo's portion of the rancho had been offered for sale although Davis had cautioned his mother-in-law against what he deemed an unwise move.

Time brought many changes. Since the early 1860s, farmers had been displaying their excellent products at annual Alameda County Fairs. The *Contra Costa Gazette* of August 16, 1862, informed its readers that the tobacco crop of Messrs. Stout and Peden of San Ramon Valley had matured beautifully. Because this was experimental, only twelve acres had been planted. Magnificent orchards, vineyards and vast expanses of grain spread throughout Alameda County especially south of San Leandro Creek where during the mission period, these fertile lowlands served merely as grazing land. Coal and copper mines in Contra Costa and Alameda Counties were of special interest to the diarist and his brothers, who occasionally visited the mines in the vicinity of Mt. Diablo. They usually traveled by stage from San Leandro to the ferry-depot in Oakland where they boarded another stage that followed the

"Telegraph Road," thence through "Big Cañon" to Lafayette's Exchange Hotel. After changing horses, the vehicle continued through excellent farming lands to Clayton, a small mining community near the base of Mt. Diablo. Here another line connected Clayton with the settlement of Martinez, the site of Ygnacio Martinez's embarcadero on the south shore of Carquinez Strait. Occasionally, J.M. and his brothers rode horseback to Clayton by way of Dublin where they acquired fresh mounts, and after a night's rest, followed a less traveled roadway through San Ramon Valley that also led to the mining area.

J.M.'s *Journal for 1867* reveals that duties assigned to him by his mother and Mr. Ward left little time for leisure. He was an avid reader, especially of the classics. Besides maintaining the family's "Milk Ranch" on the low hills a little south of San Leandro Creek, he rounded up cattle, sold small lots of land and occasionally drove a wagon to Crow Canyon to purchase thirty cords of wood for his mother. In October, after having worked all morning in the fields, he was sent to Mr. William Smith, a wholesale butcher at the Washington Market in San Francisco to sell cattle for his brother, Vicente, and Mr. Ward. Vicente, he wrote, sold his cattle on the hoof for $35.00 per head. If his mother wished to go visiting in Santa Clara County, Oakland or to El Rancho Pinole, J.M. was obliged to pack her luggage and drive the surrey. However, these journeys were often rewarding. Dona Estudillo occasionally stopped to visit friends who had comely daughters of whom J.M. was especially fond. His sisters also demanded much of his time by insisting he accompany them on shopping sprees to San Francisco. There were packages to be carried and an ice-cream parlor to be enjoyed before the exhausted boy and his sisters returned to San Leandro.

Years rolled on, each filled with the vicissitudes of life itself. The exact site of Juana Estudillo's grave has not been established despite the efforts of several interested. She rests on a gentle slope in Mount Calvary Cemetery, north of Fairmont Hospital and a little beyond the dead end of Vann Avenue. Her record of burial is believed to have been destroyed by fire. Regular interrments at Mount Calvary ceased after 1913, when Holy Sepulchre Cemetery in Hayward was opened.

The passing of loved ones was accepted as the will of God, but in 1882, prayers failed to ease a heartbreak deemed greater than death by all but one of Juana's surviving children. On March 13, 1882, our diarist, Jesus Maria Estudillo married Mrs. Mary Eckfield Tillinghast, a beautiful, twenty-three year old divorcee, who with her little daughter, Ynez, had boarded at the Estudillo House. This marriage astounded J.M.'s sisters, especially Dolores, because Mrs. Tillinghast had been baptized in the Methodist Faith. Dolores well-remembered how much J.M. disapproved of her marriage to Mr. Charles H. Cushing in 1864 only because he was a Protestant. [J.M. Estudillo, *Journal for 1864*.] Magdalena Nugent, who reputedly was the most devout Catholic in the family, was even more shocked. J.M. had been baptized and educated in the Catholic faith, and as a young man, had vehemently scorned all other religions, especially the Methodist. That her brother would marry a divorcee and "live in sin" was incredible. This union would indeed have sickened J.M's mother who abhorred even trifling deviations from the commands of the Holy Catholic Church.

In 1947, many years after the Estudillo Mansion was no longer occupied by members of the family and later by tenants, the historic structure was razed to accommodate a new St. Leander's Church and Parish House. During the demolition of the dwelling, which was still in good repair, the writer watched portions of stained-glass windows and fine redwood timbers fall on rose bushes, lilacs, lemon verbena, peonies and other ornamental plants that had defied time and neglect. Among the debris lay a section of mahogany railing that had edged the narrow, curving stairway leading from the rear of the main entrance to the lower floor which was slightly below ground level. This piece of mahogany was typed "J. Nugent" and was undoubtedly carved by the Nugents' only son, John. Within a week the entire area was cleared of all debris and every stately tree that had added so much charm to the old homestead.

The mile-long stretch of locust trees planted by Mr. John B. Ward along present Estudillo Avenue in 1866, were removed upon the widening of the thoroughfare, often referred to as merely "The Avenue." Parking meters have displaced iron hitching posts which had been placed in the shade of blossoming trees. Apartment houses, large medical buildings, and varied places of business now occupy the sites of handsome Victorian homes, where spacious gardens graced by quaint summerhouses, garden statuary and splashing fountains. Modern homes edge portions of San Leandro Creek. As one views this gentle-flowing creek, it is difficult to envision raging waters crushing squatters' cabins along its banks and the inundation of great portions of San Leandro during the winters of 1850, 1861, and early 1862. A large, concrete bridge spans the creek where early travelers were occasionally obliged to await the lowering of the stream or until the old, covered bridge of 1862 had been repaired. Wild doves and linnets still nest in the elms, bay and laurel trees, where in 1852, our diarist and Bishop Alemany strolled during Jose Joaquin Estudillos's afternoon naps.

Attractive homes now stand atop and in the folds of the city's foothills from which Pedro Fages and Father Juan Crespi and their group companies, with a guard of soldiers had studied the shoreline of San Francisco Bay in 1772.

The silence of one-time el Rodeo de Arroyo de San Leandro has been replaced by a constant hum of traffic and the drone of airliners winging their way to and from the Oakland and San Francisco terminals. Streets perpetuate the names of Jose Joaquin Estudillo, his wife, Juana Maria del Carmen Martinez, their children, some of their grandchildren, early squatters including Jacob Wright Harlan, and several of Alameda County's early citizens. Alvarado Street was named in honor of the governor from whom Estudillo received his grant, and Callan Avenue, in honor of Rev. James Callan, the first pastor of St. Leander's church.

5

Journal for 1862

San Francisco.

Wednesday, January 1, 1862.

"A happy New Year. Went to eight o'clock mass at St. Ignatius church, came home and got ready to go out visiting. My first visit was to Miss Delphine Alvarado; she was not at home. After, I met Miss Harriett Cobb. We had a very pleasant time. After calling on Miss Cobb, I called on Mrs. Townsend and Joys, here I saw Clara Cronly. My next visit was to Miss Hart where I stayed about an hour; we were alone till Mr. Mahony and Tomkins came in when I left. Came home and did not go out again."

At the onset of the Civil War, California was thrown upon her own resources, her wealth derived from industry, agriculture and commerce due to the greater demand for her products by the eastern states. In 1860 and '61, the silver mines in the Territory of Nevada were worked to capacity. Foundries and freight lines were also busy meeting appeals from Copperopolis in Tuolumne County, the nation's main source of copper during the war. [Paden & Schlichtmann, *The Big Oak Flat Road to Yosemite*, p. 59.] In later 1861, San Francisco had about 90,000 inhabitants. During the following year its population increased rapidly. While the east suffered from the war, San Francisco's plush cultural world and business climate flourished. In January of 1862, however, disaster struck.

It had been raining in California almost incessantly since the latter part of November, 1861. The city's periodicals carried accounts of state-wide destruction and suffering, and appealed to the more fortunate families to contribute money, clothing, food and other necessities for the stricken areas, mainly in the San Joaquin and Sacramento Valleys where great portions had been under water since December 19, 1861. Contributions were to be left at designated stations and shipped up the Sacramento River. Not since the winter of 1849-'50, when human bodies were found in the mud of Montgomery Street, had San Francisco witnessed such disaster.

J.M. spent most of the holiday season in the city. "Home" was wherever he chanced to find it—at a leading hotel or with his sister, Maria Magdalena Nugent on Howard Street. Unfortunately, the first young lady he called upon on New Year's Day was not at home. Delfina and her brother, Juan, lived with their parents, ex-Governor Juan Bautista Alvarado and his wife, the former Maria Martina Castro, in a stately home at 418 Greenwich Street. [Langley's *San Francisco Directory and Business Guide,* 1862-1863.]

January 2

"All day in the city. This evening I went to the theater with Edward Palmer, we had a splendid time. I saw at the theater Miss Landers and another lady from the Convent. The play was 'The Marble Heart.' It was played magnificently. Everything was over at twelve. Today Palmer, Duffy and myself went to the Willows. I was a little unfortunate. I tore my coat."

"The Marble Heart" appeared at Maguire's Opera House located on the north side of Washington Street between Montgomery and Kearny. Miss Alice Landers was the daughter of Mr. John Landers, who, with a partner, had operated a small hotel in 1849, and by 1861 was a prosperous dealer in liquors at his sizeable establishment at the junction of Market and Geary Streets.

Jesus Maria was joined by Edward Palmer, his closest friend, and Thomas Duffy, a fellow boarding student at Santa Clara College, in visiting The Willows on Valencia. It was the city's most popular gathering place for families and young people, with its spacious lawns and shade trees. There is little doubt, however, that the three young men would have found the park in a sad condition due to the rain.

January 3.

"Came to San Leandro, passed over on the one o'clock boat. Lola came with me. Palmer also came over at the same time. We had a very bad time in getting to San Leandro—the roads were very bad, we walked part of the way. Palmer stopped here tonight, we played some games and then went to bed. This was about nine o'clock when we retired, we did so because we had gone to bed at one or two all the time these past four or five days."

Jesus Maria's sister, Maria Dolores Gertrudis was nicknamed Lola. He enjoyed her company more than any other family member perhaps because of her vivaciousness, and that she was his only unmarried sister.

January 4.

"At San Leandro all day. Palmer went to the Mission (San Jose), his cousin was in the stage. I went out shooting, I killed only two larks, did not shoot at anything else. I got an American saddle to go to Oakland tomorrow. I expect to ride Mr. Ward's race mare. This evening I went to bed rather early. I was very lonesome in the parlor (of the Estudillo House) and so went to bed. Good night. This time last year I enjoyed it very well, then I had someone to keep me company, but now I am the most lonesome fellow in the house."

Sunday, January 5.

"All my expectations were put to an end when I awoke and found it raining. Of course I could not go to Oakland to church. This day has been one of the rainest [*sic*] of the season. It poured down all day without stopping. I could not even go to Peralta's house. I remained all day at the house, read a little, but most of the time I was up and down the bar room. Palmer passed to San Francisco."

San Leandro's streets were a series of quagmires as water poured down from the foothills, gashing through orchards and fields at their base, and depositing debris at the lower level. The livery stable near the hotel, which was just a few blocks from Peralta's house, all but closed its doors. No one ventured beyond shelter unless absolutely necessary.

Conditions in the settlement worsened by the hour. On January 6, J.M. wrote: "At San Leandro all day. This day has been very windy, so much so that the shade at one end of the bar room has been thrown down and it also rained during the forenoon. The creek has been higher than it ever was before. About half past four I took Mr. Ward's mare and rode down as far as Davis' and coming back stopped at Peralta's. This evening Mr. Stoakes was in the parlor and we played cards, after which I went to my room and wrote some things I had to write.

High winds and the force of San Leandro Creek began to uproot shrubbery and young trees along its banks. By noon of the same day Montgomery, Market, First, Second and Third Streets in San Francisco were under water, forcing many merchants to abandon their establishments until the water receded. Misery throughout California mounted by the hour despite occasional blue skies.

January 7.

"A beautiful day, the sky clear, of which I took the opportunity this afternoon of taking a short ride up in the hills. John Brady also went. I rode Morgan and he rode Rockey [*sic*] Mountains. We saw many quail above the tunnel. Cound not go to see the sulfur spring above the Rancheria on account of the road by the creek having caved in, we could not go any farther, came home. This evening Mr. Stoakes was in the parlor and we had some games."

W. Halley's *Centennial Book* contains the data concerning the tunnel visited by J.M. and his companion. For the year, 1860, it reads: "Mr. J.B. Ward, agent of the Estudillo Rancho, bored a 500 foot tunnel in the hills through which runs the San Leandro Creek, to make a reservoir for irrigating the land below, near the place where the Contra Costa Water Company has lately bored a much larger one and constructed a very large reservoir." This was named Lake Chabot in honor of Mr. Anthony Chabot, the company's first president.

January 9.

"We got up at ten o'clock. This day is worth to be recorded in this journal and in the annals of San Leandro for the overflow of San Leandro Creek. The water began to rise about eleven o'clock and by one, all of Davis' place was inundated. The water came out first above Lola's old residence and from there down on both sides of the creek for about a mile, was a sheet of water. The damage done to some of the poor families near the creek was very great and this evening a family who lived at the Landing (the Estudillos' embarcadero) has stopped at the hotel. The daughter's house of the butcher was carried away. This evening it is still raining and most likely the creek will rise again."

January 10.

"This morning was very cloudy and gave the appearance of rain but we did not have any. My first attraction this morning was to go and see the bridge, which was in a very dangerous position on account of one of the middle piers having been swept away. The creek last night was two feet higher than the day before yesterday, but it is lowering fast. A very dull day, very little business done at the house."

The damage to the bridge caused stage travel to be temporarily discontinued. Exceptionally high tides compelled the ferry boats, "Oakland" and "Contra Costa" to alter their schedules. San Lorenzo Creek changed its course several times as it gashed great portions from its banks. Hundreds of cattle and sheep perished in deep, sticky mud as the unusually high tides of San Francisco Bay extended the flooded area eastward to present Hesperian Boulevard. Despite the repair, the covered bridge at San Leandro Creek remained a source of concern until May 1864, when it was replaced by a sturdier structure.

Sunday, January 12.

"In San Leandro till half-past two when I left on my way to the College, came to Oakland in time for the last boat but my intention was to remain in Oakland tonight. The roads were very bad. . . . Came straight to Mr. Nugent's, Magdalena was sick, had been for three or four days . . ."

Magdalena was expecting her first child, but may not have spoken of her condition in the presence of her youngest brother. On the evening of January 12, word arrived in San Francisco that the misery and destruction of properties in the Sacramento and San Joaquin Valleys had reached almost unbelievable proportions. Despite the late hour, San Franciscans immediately set to work gathering more supplies for the stricken area and by midnight of the following day, two steamers carrying thirty tons of cooked food, twenty-two tons of clothing and bedding and several thousand dollars made their way up the Sacramento River.

January 13.

"In San Francisco all day. Went to the thirty mile race. Palmer was there also, we went together to the city. Alviso's horse won the race, the other horse did not run the last mile, gave out. Time; one hour and twenty-eight minutes. This evening I went to the theater, Maguire's. I saw there Ed. Palmer, Jas. Hughes, Guin and others. I took with me Mr. Nugent's dagger when I went to the theater for which I was very sorry afterwards. I was scolded by my mother for having taken the dagger. They looked for it and couldn't find it."

J.M. gave no reason for taking Mr. Nugent's "dagger," a gentleman's bowie-knife, still worn by some Californians as a weapon of defense. By 1862, few male inhabitants of San Francisco deemed it necessary to wear any kind of weapon unless they frequented, or were obliged to be in the vicinity of the rougher neighborhoods. Mr. Nugent, however, was never without a small pistol even in the respectable areas of the city. Although J.M. frequently wrote of arriving home "at a very late hour," he rarely divulged where he spent his time. It remains somewhat doubtful if he and his companions practiced slumming, as visiting this area was later known. The bawdy districts between Broadway, Pacific and Jackson Streets were named The Barbary Coast in the mid-1860s, but the worst section was mainly on Pacific Street between Kearny and Dupont. A tourist guide-book of 1871 warns travelers: "Give it a 'wide berth,'" if you value your life."

January 14.

"This morning when I got up, I first went to church but it was all over; nevertheless, I next went in and remained inside for quarter of an hour saying my prayers. I went to the Alviso boat to see some college boys go to Santa Clara."

January 16.

"This morning I slumbered till a late hour, on account that last night I was up till very late . . . This evening at supper we had a long conversation between my mother, Concepcion (Ward), Mr. Nugent, among whom I counted myself. The latter part of our parlying was about our property in the city. Mr. N. said that if Saunders (Mr. John H. Saunders) had presented our claim to the land commissioners in 1852, we would have at this day, property in San Francisco worth two and a half million dollars. Last night and all day it rained very much and it is raining whilst I am writing at twelve o'clock this evening."

January 17.

"This morning was so cold and rainy that I kept in bed till nine o'clock. I believe that almost all last night was a continual rain as it was today; it stopped at five o'clock this afternoon. The corner of Second and Market looked like a small river, how the water ran! It seems that this world is coming to an end by water."

Saturday, January 18.

"This evening before supper I went to confession. I went to St. Ignatius Church, my confessor was Father Bouchard. This afternoon I went to visit Maria but she was not at home, saw Miss Gettin. I saw Solari and Spivalo, I was in their rooms at the El Dorado. This day it did not rain very much, but nevertheless we had a shower, but last night we had rain enough to drown one-self if one happened to be out. I was also at Miss Alvarado's house, did not see her nor John, Jr. After confession I went to see Father Traverso. I also saw the President of St. Ign. This evening I went to bed earlier than usual."

Sunday, January 19.

"I went to communion. I was at half-past ten mass. Father Bouchard preached an excellent sermon. He alluded to the unhappy conditions of our country and that this war (the Civil War) will not be terminated by the sword but by calling on the name of Jesus. It had been a punishment to the United States for her many crimes, some by war and we here in California, by floods. I started to go to see Maria (Mrs. W.H. Davis) but the rain fell so hard that I determined to come back, which I did. Mr. Ward arrived today. It has been a rainy day and this evening is raining very hard, no prospects of good weather."

From November 6, 1861, through January 19, 1862, almost thirty-three inches of rain had fallen in San Francisco and about the same amount in the Sacramento and San Joaquin Valleys. San Francisco's periodicals continued their appeal for food, bedding and clothing. Medicines were now added to the list of the most needed items as countless numbers suffered from respiratory ailments. The California Steam Navigation Company's vessels, Antelope and Senator, had great difficulty in plying the Sacramento River because of poor visibility, floating cattle, wrecked dwellings, furniture and other debris. W.H. Brewer was in San Francisco on the 19th and wrote: "There have been some of the most stupendous charities I have ever seen." Each day of the week, except Sundays, a steamer left Sacramento filled to capacity with men and women carrying infants and children wrapped in bedding, draperies, or whatever dry clothing was available. Brewer added: "You can imagine the effect it must have on the finances and prosperity of the state. The end is not yet."

January 20.

". . . This evening I made up my mind to go to Sacramento tomorrow night. I was down to see Calvin. The weather looks very sad indeed, so many persons suffering up in the country and I am here detained, with hopes to get to the College sometime or other."

Mr. Calvin was one of the agents for the California Steam Navigation Company, a monopoly that controlled all the central and coastal business. The company was organized on March 4, 1854. The Senator, a side-wheeler, was the first steamboat sent around the Horn to serve on the Sacramento River and it alternated between runs up and down the river and along the coast to San Diego. The largest and best known steamers on the Sacramento River route were the Senator, Cornelia and the New World.

January 21.

"My first visit to the Queen City! This afernoon I started to Sacramento on the steamer Antelope. I took two letters of introduction to Capt. Poole, one from Mr. Ward and another from Mr. Judah (Mr. Charles Judah of Nugent [Judah, Attorneys at Law in San Francisco). The Captain treated me very well on my trip. Jose Antonio went on the steamer as far as Benicia. As the day was very rainy and also the night, I could not remain on deck and consequently did not enjoy the scenery. The steamer Nevada ran twice into us, splitting some of the stern of our boat, at this time I jumped out of bed very much scared. Arrived at Sacramento at half-past one P.M."

Captain E.A. Poole was undoubtedly courteous to the diarist, but may have been displeased that Ward and Judah had added to his responsibilities by placing an excitable, adventuresome, and somewhat irresponsible young man in his care during the 125 or more miles of this hazardous journey.

The steamer accident occurred at Steamboat Slough, a particularly sharp and dangerous bend on the Sacramento River, a short distance north from the town of Rio Vista and about sixty-two miles from San Francisco. Fourteen days later, the Nevada hit a snag at the same point and was forced against the river bank where she sprung a leak. However, all passengers were safely removed and some time later, the boat was towed to San Francisco for repairs.

January 22.

"I was up at six o'clock A.M. Had breakfast with the Captain and two other officers of the Steam Navigation Company after which I hired a small boat and went to the Capitol. I visited most of all the Chambers of the Legislature, and as a matter of course, the Senate and Assembly chambers. I saw Pacheco and Mr. Watt, the latter gave me a letter to Mr. Nugent. I was very much delighted with my trip. All of Sacramento was under water with very little exception. We came away at half past two. The Legislature adjourned to meet at San Francisco. It was a pitting [*sic*] sight to see the animals perishing by the water, cows, horses, pigs and many fowls. We arrived at San Francisco at half past nine and delightful scenery, but such a waste of waters."

Brewer visited Sacramento two months later and wrote: "The new Capitol is far out in the water—the Governor's house stands as in a lake. Not a road leading from the city is passable—many houses are partially toppled over, several streets now avenues of water, are blocked up with houses that have floated in them, dead animals lie about here and there—a dreadful picture. No description that I can write will give you any adequate conception of the discomfort and wretchedness that this must give rise to."

On January 23 and 24, J.M. visited his friends, bade farewell to the Fathers at St. Ignatius Church and assembled his books and clothing for his departure to Santa Clara College. On the 25th, he boarded an Alviso-bound vessel and chatted merrily with other students. Most pleasing were the occasional coy glances from young ladies enroute to San Jose's Convent of Notre Dame, but because they were properly chaperoned, good breeding demanded he ignore their flattering attention. He was anxious to return to his classmates, the Fathers, and once again to Santa Clara and San Jose, but his arrival was not as pleasant as anticipated.

6

Return to Santa Clara College

January 25, 1862

"Came to San Jose on my way to the College. I was introduced to Miss Alma Hall by Mr. Folger (a prominent Oakland merchant), we had a pleasant trip on the steamer; but then from Alviso up to San Jose the passengers had to walk about two miles, I among the rest. Miss Hall and myself stopped at Crandell's (Hotel in San Jose). This evening we played cards in the parlor, after we had played for some time, a young man from the Protestant College came in and we played still longer. When I went to my room I wrote a letter to my mother. This evening it was very cold indeed."

William H. Brewer, who with his associates traveled this route about one month later, wrote: "We took the steamer to Alviso, at the end of San Francisco Bay, then by stage for seven miles to San Jose. The roads were awful. We loaded up, six stages full, in the rain, and had scarcely gone a hundred rods when the wheels sank to their axles and the horses nearly to their bellies in the mud, where we unloaded. Then the usual strife on such occasion. Horses get down, driver swears, passengers get in the mud, put shoulders to the wheels and extricate the vehicle. We walk aways, then get in, ride two miles, then get out and walk two more in the deepest, stickiest, worst mud you ever saw, the rain pouring. I hardly knew which grew the heaviest, my muddy boots or my wet overcoat. Then we ride again, then walk again, and finally ride into town, having made the seven miles in four hours."

Sunday, January 26.

"Had breakfast at nine and soon after I came to Santa Clara on foot.

Ramon Pico acted very badly, he promised to let me have a horse and today he told me that a wagon or stage was going to Santa Clara, now this was a lie; he said this because he did not let me have the horse. I went to see the Fathers and afterwards the boys. Many have not come back yet. I went out and visited Dona Soledad and asked Luis Arguello for a horse, he told me that he had no riding horse, nor saddle, after which I went to see the President of the Seminary to let him know that Miss Hall was at San Jose. I stopped with L. Arguello. Molina was there, we had a splendid punch made at the house before bed. It rained this evening."

Jose Ramon Pico was about fifty-three years of age and the son of Andres Pico and had acquired through his uncle, Pio Pico, Mexican-California's last governor, extensive holdings formerly the property of Mission Santa Clara. Jose Ramon probably did not know that stage travel had been temporarily discontinued and owing to road conditions, no other vehicles were available. J.M.'s three mile walk from San Jose to the college was undoubtedly very disagreeable.

One can well imagine J.M.'s disgust when Luis Arguello also refused him a horse, probably for the same reason that Ramon Pico did not extend the favor. J.M. was notorious for mistreating his horses. In July, 1864, he rented a horse from Martin and Baker Stables in San Jose and rode about fifteen miles in one hour and twenty minutes. In his *Journal for 1864,* he wrote that it was a very warm day and that much to his displeasure, his return took him ten minutes longer. His brother, Jose Antonio, was even less considerate. Upon one occasion he mounted a horse at Rancho San Leandro to visit El Rancho Pinole. After his departure, J.M. wrote: "I can well imagine in what condition he will bring the horse back, the same if not worse than the last time."

Although Luis Arguello, the son of California's first governor under Mexican rule (who died in 1830), was about fourteen years older than J.M., he frequently entertained him and a few of his classmates. When J.M. arrived at his home on February 26, Luis was entertaining Zaccharias Molina, a son of Ciriaco Molina, who, in 1849, had been employed to drive a herd of sheep from New Mexico to California. After making his home in various settlements, Ciriaco established a permanent home in San Jose.

January 27.

"Wrote a letter to my mother from San Jose and another to Miss Hall, the latter I did not post, I kept it. This day is worthy of being distinguished for the great snow storm that has covered the mountains and to some extent, the valleys. I rode on horseback this morning to San Jose and when I got there I found Miss Hall had left the Hotel and gone to some friend's house. I could not know where she could be, and therefore I determined to be away. I fetched my valise on my horse. I had a hard time getting to the college. This afternoon I arranged all my books and desk, formerly Solari's and remained in the study room the last hour. Also this evening I studied with the rest of the boys."

Among the books J.M. studied during the early 1860s are: "A Compendium of Natural Philosophy," "Manual of Minerology," "Grammar of Rhetoric and Polite Literature," "A Manual of Chemistry," "Elements of Algebra," and "Analytical and Practical Grammar of the English Language." These are presently in the archives of the University of Santa Clara. Students were usually not permitted to read books other than those required for their subjects with the exception of approved classics and those in the institution's extensive library. Books received as gifts had to meet the approval of the President.

January 28.

"First day I went to class. I made a composition in the English class. Commenced today in chemistry on Metallic elements. The last study hours I spent putting down some scraps in my scrap book. This day has been extremely cold. The snow still appears on the mountains. The ice was very thick this morning. After dinner (noon) I went to Father Mengarini's room and gave him one hundred and fifty dollars on account for my tuition. Molina received Solari's letter and wished me to pay him eight dollars for the desk; but I would not give him but six."

Father Gregory Mengarini, S.J., was among the missionaries that accompanied John Bidwell from the Kansas River to California in 1841 [Gloria Ricci Lothrop, p. 53, *Recollections of the Flathead Mission, the Memories of Fr. Gregory Mengarini, S.J.*]. Father Mengarini was sent from Rome because of his virtues, his great facility with languages, and his knowledge of medicine and music. In 1862, he served as the Treasurer of Santa Clara College.

J.M.'s chemistry classes were held in the three-story Science Building erected in 1861. The finest scientific equipment in the west was used and it housed one of the most complete in the entire nation.

January 30.

"This afternoon it rained a little. As a matter of course, today we did not have school, during the study hour of ten, we had our debate. I did not prepare a speech because I had not been here long enough and did not know the subject to debate on; but nevertheless, I spoke something on metals. This subject was whether the use of animals was more useful than that of metals. The negative won; metals. For our next debate; Was the Maid of Orleans Executed Justly or Not. I was put on the negative. Tonight it was extremely cold."

In 1862, there were two debating societies at Santa Clara College. Young Estudillo was the secretary of the Philhistorian Society. Its president was Reverend E.M. Nattini, S.J.; John Henry Moses Townsend was Vice-President; Thomas Van Ness was Treasurer; and Albert Faure; the Censor. The Philatelic Debating Society's 1862 officers were: Reverend E. Young, S.J., President; Robert Keating, Vice-President; Bernard D. Murphy, Recording Secretary; James Breen, Corresponding Secretary; G. Henning, Treasurer; Augustus Bowie, Librarian; and James Hughes, Censor. According to the Rev. Father Arthur D. Spearman, S.J., the Philatelic Debating Society was organized on February 22, 1857. The officers for that year were: The Rev. Michael Accolti, S.J., Moderator; Master W. Rowe, Vice-President; Frank Bray, Treasurer; John Bary, Secretary; and John M. Burnett, Censor.

January 31.

"Class as usual, but again our teacher is changed in our arithmetic class from Father Veyret to Mr. Sullivan. It is almost provoking for one to have his teacher changed so often, but it cannot be helped. We had composition in history. I was also examined which I did not expect on account of not having been here long enough. Today I took a good deal of exercise playing ball. It deserves being noticed that we had a respectable dinner, and hope they'll continue doing the same hereafter. The weather this afternoon is quite pleasant, not as cold as yesterday."

Father F. Veyret, S.J. was Professor of Mathematics, Astronomy and Spanish. Mr. Sullivan was one of the assistant lay teachers. On dark, chilly mornings, the diarist frequently looked out of his dormitory window to view the distant mountains still dotted with patches of snow, and wondered when they would resume their emerald beauty. On January 31, W.H. Brewer wrote that the weather in San Francisco had also cleared up, but "All the roads in the middle of the state are impassable, so all mails are cut off. . . . In the Sacramento Valley for some distance the tops of the (telegraph) poles are under water."

Sunday, February 2.

"I went to communion. The ceremony of blessing the candles was performed. F. Prelato officiating. Today was the feast of Incarnation, we had no study in the morning nor catechism this afternoon. I spent most of the time at playing ball at Rounders, our side won one game, and this was for a dollar of candy; we played them again, and had to stop the game on account of rain which commenced about three P.M. The weather gives the appearance of a good deal of rain just setting in as before."

The candy was purchased from a small contribution made by each of the players, bought from the small store on the campus operated by the Fathers. Students were not permitted to carry money about their person, but were permitted a small sum occasionally from a deposit they had given to the college treasurer at the beginning of each semester. Twenty-five cents a week per student was deemed an ample amount for candy or cookies. A slightly larger sum was permitted for special occasions, but had to meet the approval of Fathers Villiger and Caredda, President and Vice-President of the College.

February 3.

"They say that 'health is nature's wealth.' Without health is natural bankruptcy. This very day last year, one of our fellow students departed [from] this world, John Rollston, and at this time there is not one confined to his bed in the Infirmary, thank God for it. Last night and early this morning it rained very much; but during the day it only kept cloudy, but this evening it poured down at a furious rate for a time and then it cleared out and did not rain any more. This morning we had composition in Geography. At breakfast I received the *Sacramento Daily Union*. During the evening's study hour I made part of my composition for Wednesday. In Philosophy I made two problems."

An entry in J.M.'s *Journal for 1861* on February 3, confirms that he was very fond of John Rollston. "With grief and consternation I will put down on this page the death of one of our fellow students, name is John Rollston, he died this morning at half past eight o'clock, he had only been confined to his bed six days, his death is very much lamented by all but he died a happy death, all the Sacraments were administered to him."

February 5, 1862, was a delightful day, but uneventful. On the following day he wrote: "This afternoon we had the monthly places and I was fifth in Philosophy, 8th in English, 9th in History, 4th in Geography, 7th in Arithmetic. These places no doubt are low, but this part of the session I lost a month and another month the first part of the session. I could not expect better places. In Chemistry class we did not recite any lesson but Father Messick gave us to write a lecture on gasses, allowed one week and half of time to do it. It rained this morning very hard but stopped at eleven o'clock A.M."

February 7.

"We had a tolerable good dinner, a little better than last Friday, although the one last week was pretty good. We hope they shall continue to do the same hereafter. This morning F. Caredda commenced to examine our English class and also the arithmetic. We had Elocution class. I spoke the Speech of Gratten in the Irish Parliament. I was told by Father Young [Professor of English Literature and Elocution] that I had improved in my voice. This day I made a resolution of studying my grammar and arithmetic more than any other study."

February 8.

"This morning I was examined in grammar and arithmetic, as for the former, I stood a middling examination, but for the latter, I passed much better than English. We had Philosophy and some experiments performed on Liquids or Non-Elastic Fluids in motion. Today we had a short drill. I was nominated and elected 2nd Corporal by acclamation, at first I did not wish to accept the office but afterwards I consented, not that I cared for the office. Palmer went to the Mission [San Jose], promised to come back tomorrow."

Sunday, February 9.

"Did not have the office of Sodality, but we had a study during that time. John Burnett was here this morning and Augustus Spivalo was here in the afternoon. I only saluted him, had not the opportunity of speaking to him. This afternoon we had catechism, I was not asked anything. F. Veyret related some facts. I played a good deal of ball. This evening I got from F. Bosco [Father Aloysius Bosco, S.J.] five express envelopes. It has been a beautiful day, but this morning it was very cold. Today we had some visitors, first we had for a long time. Mr. Rayland [Ryland] and another gentleman."

John M. Burnett was a son of the Honorable Peter H. Burnett who resigned as Governor of California in 1851 and moved to San Jose where the family resided in a magnificent home surrounded by spacious gardens. Later, in the same year, Mr. Burnett resumed the practice of law in San Jose with his two sons-in-law, Messrs. Wallace and Ryland. John M. Burnett entered Santa Clara College as a boarding student in 1851.

February 10.

"I heard from Palmer that snow had destroyed all the grass around the Mission where his father's sheep are kept and about fifty had died, many cattle also had died. I hope this has not been the case at San Joaquin."

San Joaquin was Juana Estudillo's inherited part of Rancho El Pinole to which she added, by purchase, with acreage from her sisters. Edward Palmer's father had requested the President of the college, the Rev. Burchard Villiger, S.J. to grant leave to his son for a few days so that he could help in caring for the new lambs that demanded special attention during the extremely cold weather. On February 12, J.M received mail and newspapers which had been delayed by several days due to road conditions. He read his letter from Lola, and then he sent a valentine to Miss Cobb. By the time he had resumed his studies, great clouds again hovered over the valley obscuring the distant snow-capped mountains. Another deluge was inevitable. Before turning off his lamp for the night, J.M. paused at his window to view the drenched land and then wrote: "God help the poor sufferers."

February 17.

"Received the *Union* this evening. This afternoon there was a great excitement in town, flags being halled [*sic*] up, firing cannons, and many reports of guns, on account of the great Federal Victory of fifteen thousand men taken prisoners and a great fort at Tennessee. Also there prevailed great enthusiasm among the boys to know the news. . . ."

The excitment was justified. On February 12, Brigadier General Ulysses S. Grant, at the head of fifteen thousand men, moved from the recently captured Fort Henry to Fort Donelson in Tennessee. Four days later, Genral Buckner of the Confederate forces surrendered Fort Donelson. Grant later wrote that the victory had ". . . the greatest number of prisoners of the war ever taken in any battle on this continent."

John Laird Wilson, in his *Pictorial History of the Great Civil War* relates: "Here one finds that during the early part of the Civil War, heavily-armed Confederate vessels began to prey upon the commerce of the North. One was the *Savannah,* a schooner of fifty tons. In early June 1861, the vessel succeeded in eluding the blockading squadron off Charleston and captured a Union craft laden with sugar for Philadelphia. About one month later, the *Savannah* was captured by the United States' brig-of-war *Perry* and was obliged to surrender. The only notation J.M made of the Civil War in his *Journal for 1861,* is that he had heard of "some trouble in the Eastern states," then deemed a far-distant land.

On December 20, 1864, while J.M. was enjoying the social life of Virginia City's elite society, an iron-clad vessel also bearing the name *Savannah* and flying a Confederate Flag, was blown up by the retreating Confederates the day before the city of Savannah, Georgia was surrendered to General Sherman. Two days later, the general wrote to President Lincoln: "I beg to present you, as a Christmas gift, the city of Savannah, with 150 heavy guns and plenty of ammunition, and also about 25,000 bales of cotton." This was the Union's first major victory during the Civil War.

February 19.

"Today news came that Savannah was taken by the Federals and great excitement prevailed in Santa Clara and in this college. This afternoon I went to see Father Accolti to ask him for a scapulary, had none but was going to procure some from the Sisters at San Jose."

During the Civil War rumors and misinformation frequently reached California. W.H. Brewer was in San Francisco in February, 1982, but no mention appears in his pocket journal regarding the false report which he brought throughout Santa Clara County. The City of Savannah, Georgia was not taken by the Federals until December 21, 1864.

The "Sisters at San Jose" were the instructors at the Convent of Notre Dame which was located a short distance to the southeast of Santa Clara. Students of Santa Clara College were not permitted to visit the institution unless by invitation from a Sister and permission from the President of the College. While visiting, they were constantly under the supervision of one of the Sisters, except when the visit took place in the convent's parlor or garden and an adult relative accompanied them.

February 20.

"This morning we had no study, the cadets drilled most of the time. I collected from the company about nine dollars, sent out to get the powder and caps for the 22nd and this afternoon we also had no study, the time of study was allowed to us to clean our muskets. I and Bowie made a great number of cartridges. This evening during the study hour we had our debate, our side won. Our next debate; 'resolved that the name *great* was better deserved to Constantine than to Theodosius.' I was appointed to speak on the affair. The meeting adjourned very abruptly."

The Santa Clara Cadets was organized on May 8, 1856, but in 1862, the name was changed to Stanford Cadets in honor of Leland Stanford, who served as Governor of California from January, 1862 to December, 1863. Early in 1862, the governor sent the cadets forty old Springfield rifles to be used for drilling and parading through Santa Clara and San Jose.

Among the cadets was Ensign James F. Breen, a son of Patrick Breen, a survivor of the ill-fated Donner Party of 1846. About two years after his arrival in California, Patrick acquired a large, two-story adobe structure constructed in 1840 for General Jose Castro, who served as Acting Governor of Alta California from September, 1835 to January, 1836. The Castro adobe served as his administrative office and housed his secretary. At present the large adobe structure and rear courtyard is located in the town of San Juan Bautista.

February 22.

"It has never been known to have rained on the 22nd, ever since this college is put up twelve years ago. I am sorry to say that all our expectations of turning out with the company were banished when we got up, it was raining very hard and continued so for all the day and evening. I went with the Philathic [sic] Debating Society to see the exhibition of the other college (the Methodist institution). I saw Miss Hall who read a composition, subject, "Washington." We were all very much displeased with the insulting speech of one of the speakers, I mean that he insulted all the Catholics, after having invited F. Young to sit among the Trustees.

We had our exhibition this afternoon, very few people here, there was only one woman. It rained all during the performance. The Debate between Murphy and Keating was very good; Is a Republic the Best Form of Government? A dialogue by J. Hughes was very good, 'The Correspondent.' We had an excellent dinner, of course no study this evening."

Unknown to J.M., on this day Jefferson Davis was inaugurated as President of the Confederate Government. This event and the news of various bloody engagements taking place in the East wouldn't have reached California until much later.

It is not surprising that so few people attended the exercises at Santa Clara College. Road conditions had worsened in part because nearby Guadalupe Creek had again overflowed. W.H. Brewer intended to board the Alviso boat on March 3rd. He wrote: "We got within two miles and a half of the boat, where we found a stream had broken over its banks and had made a new bed and had cut up the road so that it was impossible to get across with the stages. After much delay a part of the passengers got across on the backs of horses, some getting down, and all thoroughly wet."

February 24.

"There is a saying in Spanish which says; 'El Lunes ni las gallinas ponen,' meaning that on Mondays hens do not lay eggs. It has been a dull day, cloudy and gloomy. S. Purdy was here this afternoon, he was looking for some recruits for his regiment where he is 2nd Lieut. He had his full uniform and put on many airs. Boyle went out with him. This evening I learned perfectly well how to measure gulfs, countries, etc. with the use of the scale."

Two days later, J.M.'s friends, John Roche of Bodega and J.P.K. Cunningham of Michigan Bluff, a small community on the north fork of the American River, were promoted to higher classes, and for the first time during the spring semester, J.M. smoked a "Cigarrito." Smoking positively was prohibited at the college, and because he was profoundly conscientious and abided by all rules, he probably smoked the small, narrow cigar well beyond the campus. Students were permitted to walk towards San Jose but only as far as the bridge over Los Gatos Creek. One tenth of a mile beyond this was the Guadalupe Creek bridge which the faculty deemed too near the Convent of Notre Dame. Special permission was occasionally granted if one or more students wished to purchase books or other items at A. Waldteufel Book and Stationary Store located on the Murphy Block in San Jose. However, students were warned not to loiter in the settlement or in the vicinity of the convent or in any way attract attention either by singing, whistling, laughter, or speaking to any young lady who chanced to be in the convent gardens. Upon their return from San Jose, all purchases, especially reading matter, were checked before students entered the dormitory.

The town of San Jose had flourished since 1849 and like most of California's early settlements, it had its share of gambling dens, saloons, gun-play, and undesirables. By the late 1850s, San Jose had attained some respectability. Despite the increasing number of reputable places of business and substantial families, it was some time before the settlement was entirely cleansed of crime and ill-famed establishments. Upon the onset of the Civil War, it became a hotbed of Secessionists who voiced their heated opinions wherever they chose. The town's 7000 inhabitants were mainly Mexican and Spanish Californians, many of whom were uneducated and listened for curiosity, but there were also many Americans who favored the South. Brewer wrote: "There were many more Secessionists in this state than you in the east believe, and many of them are desperados ready for anything in the shape of a row." [W.H. Brewer, *op cit.,* p. 176.] This was why the Faculty of Santa Clara College discouraged visits to San Jose, fearing that students might innocently become involved in a skirmish which could develop into a battle. However, students who could prove they were to visit a well-known family or meet a relative at Mr. Crandell's hotel were given permission, but required to return before the evening meal.

February 28.

"We had permission today to talk at dinner, John M. Burnett dined with us. We had our debate this evening, the decision was given in favor of the affirmative; for the next debate, 'Resolved, that the opening of the Chinese ports was beneficial to that country or not.' It was agreed to have a public debate at some future time."

February 28.

"When I came to the study room for Chemistry class, I found two letters in my desk, one from my mother and another from Dolores. Lola (Dolores) tells me that she has been very sick, that they did not expect her to live. Of course these sad news pierced my heart at the first sight. . . . We had speaking class. I spoke, 'Unfurl the banner of freedom.' We had in chemistry class a lecture by Roche and soda water was made. I took a glass of it, it was very good. I got this afternoon the 'Spectator' from the library, I commenced reading it this evening. Lola tells me that Dona Estudillo [is] not pleased with my epistolary style, that I have not improved my English. Indeed, I am very sorry that she has such a bad opinion of me, also says that I spent too much money on my way to the college."

J.M. always resented being reprimanded by his mother or any instructor at the college especially in the presence of other students. Students of J.M.'s heritage and Castilian pride were at times difficult to handle and made to understand that corrections were not intended as personal affronts. Some would leave a classroom without fully understanding the subject rather than ask a question or admit that he did not understand a subject in the presence of his classmates.

March 4.

"Had compositions in all my morning classes. This afternoon we did not have any chemistry class, but one hour to study, and then got ready to go out in town to see the panorama. Many Fathers went, and they were not pleased with the songs of a lady who sang, so they appeared to be, and many did express his sentiments. The [stereoptican] views were very good, we remained two hours and half seating in the hall. During the first study time I wrote two pages and half of my composition for tomorrow, a letter to an absent friend."

March 5.

"Wrote a letter to my mother and also received one from Dolores. Today the First days of Lent have begun, being Ash Wednesday we received ashes on our heads. We have a dispensation from the Archbishop [Alemany] to eat meat on Wednesdays and Saturdays of Lent. This afternoon we had the monthly places. I was first, equal with Roche and Duffy in catechism. I had very good places in most of my classes, I was 3rd in philosophy, 4th in chemistry. This morning I received the *Alameda Gazette*. Nothing very interesting."

In the morning of the following day, J.M. studied and wrote letters and in the afternoon he and Luis Arguello drove about Santa Clara in a carriage, but before he returned to the college, he visited Miss Soledad. It remains doubtful if he gave any thought to the many volunteers of his age who were engaged in the bloody battles of the Civil War which by this time, had developed to great intensity. On March 6 President Lincoln proposed to Congress the gradual compensated emancipation of the border-states' slaves. On the same day, W.H. Brewer had returned from Sacramento. He wrote: "Houses, stores, stables, everything were surrounded by water. Yards were ponds enclosed by tables, sofas, the fragments of houses were floating in the muddy waters or lodged in nooks and corners. . . ." Only portions of San Francisco and San Jose were inundated, but misery among the poorer classes mounted as the rains continued.

March 15.

"Lecture this morning on the sixth commandment by Father Masnata [Professor of Ancient Language]. After dinner we had a general drill and it was proposed that we should go to San Jose on St. Patrick's Day. This evening after beads [evening rosary in the students' chapel], our debating Society met to dispose of some business left undone at the last meeting, quite an exciting time it was during the meeting. . . . This evening there was an appearance of rain."

Sunday, March 16.

"Last night it rained very much and this morning the ground was very wet, so much so that some thought the cadets would not be able to turn out tomorrow. The whole of the day was cloudy and giving the appearance of rain. . . . After supper the cadets fell into ranges and we went to see Father Caredda to let us go to San Jose tomorrow, but we could not get his permission. During the evening's study I wrote my composition and my manuscript of a letter to Mr. Ward."

". . . Our breakfast was not so good as expected by the boys, but dinner was tolerable [*sic*] good. The afternoon was so beautiful that the cadets went and paraded in town, we fired about sixteen or seventeen times, only twenty of rank and file turned out, they did pretty well, but plenty of mud in the streets. After leaving our muskets in the armory, Father Caredda called all the cadets to the gymnasium where he treated us with good California wine and cakes; this he did he said, because the cadets had not gone into Cameron's [Hotel] to drink what Cameron offered. Indeed we praise the action of Father Caredda, and may he govern this college with the same discipline as it has been heretofore, and tonight he gave us a 'holy-night.' The boys had a dance in the gymnasium. I was not present, I remained in the study-room till half past nine P.M., then went to bed and so did the other boys who stayed up, Delmas, Van Ness, Crandell and myself."

A "holy-night" permitted students to spend their evening as they wished within the college or on the campus and was usually granted as a reward for some outstanding action on their part. In 1862, three Delmas brothers attended Santa Clara College. J.M.'s friend was Delfine M. Delmas, who entered the college in 1858 at the age of fourteen and became one of its outstanding students. At the close of the spring semester in 1862, he received the degree Artium Baccalaureus and in the following year, he received the highest of his class by having attained the Artium Magister Degree. In 1865, after his graduation from Yale University's Department of Law, Delfine returned to San Jose and became a law partner of Bernard D. Murphy in San Jose who was also graduated with high honors from Santa Clara College in 1862.

Delphine M. Delmas served as a Regent of the University of California from 1880 to 1888, when he retired. He married a daughter of Colonel Joseph P. Hoge and owned a beautiful home in San Francisco and San Jose besides a large building on his San Jose property which he named the *Paul Block* in honor of his son, Paul [*Bay of San Francisco,* Vol. 1, p. 453].

Thomas Van Ness was the son of the Honorable James Van Ness who arrived in California in 1850 and served as Mayor of San Francisco during 1855-'56. Thomas Crandell, who also studied during the evening of March 17, was a son of Mr. C.T. Crandell, the owner of San Jose's fashionable Mansion House.

Apparently Santa Clara had not been informed of the Federal victory by the capture of Manassas on March 16, which caused great excitement in San Francisco and the firing of a hundred guns in its plaza at nightfall. Brewer watched the jubilant crowds and later wrote: "I trust that the way is opened now for a speedy close of this unfortunate war."

March 18.

"Today we heard that small pox has attacked many of the citizens of San Jose and the greatest precaution was taken in transporting goods. This afternoon Cunningham was here to visit the boys on his way to San Juan."

During the epidemic, all schools in San Jose were closed to prevent the disease from spreading to Santa Clara by students who resided in the settlement. Students who happened to be in San Jose were ordered to remain at Crandell's Hotel until Mr. Crandell and Father Caredda deemed it safe for them to return. Many of the deaths in San Jose were among the poorer families on the outskirts of the town where little or no attention was given to sanitation. Smallpox also raged in other parts of California during this period of floods and misery. Countless numbers had been stricken with pneumonia, but deaths occurred mainly among children and the aged.

March 21.

"Received this morning in a envelope, a letter from my mother, another from Dolores and five dollars. Lola tells me that Mr. Ward has been very busy with cases in court and was very scarce of money, that for that reason he did not send the amount I asked for. My mother rebuked me for having written a very mean letter to Juan [his brother]. This evening our Spiritual Retreat began. Father Beaudreaux commenced this evening to give us a lecture."

March 22.

"Wrote a letter to Dolores, directed it to San Francisco." Although Dolores lived with her mother in San Leandro, J.M. may have addressed the letter to the Nugents' home in San Francisco where Dolores frequently visited her sister, Magdalena. J.M.'s letter probably contained some disparaging remarks about his mother Juana Estudillo. ". . . First day of our Retreat during the recreations, I spent the time reading and meditating in the vineyard. We had three lectures today, another this evening. I may say that I kept good silence, of course not silent all the time without speaking a single word. After supper I went into Father Mengarini's room to acquaint him with the unlucky conditions Mr. Ward has met with and told him the reasons why the money has not been sent. I took to read the 'Lives of the Saints' and Challoner's 'Meditations' for every day of the year."

The vineyard was located to the southwest side of the campus and near present Varsi Hall of the University of Santa Clara, and had been planted by the neophytes of Mission Santa Clara prior to 1833. Because the area was rarely visited by other students, J.M. often chose the quiet place for his meditations, or whenever letters from San Leandro had caused him to worry about his mother's financial difficulties.

March 24.

"Third and last day of our Spiritual Retreat and this morning I made a general confession, during the recreations I had time to make a good examination of conscience in the vineyard. I was constantly meditating on these points; on hell and the glory of God, and of eternity, eternity, eternity. This afternoon I felt a little sick with sore throat, not danger. This day I shall mark out as being one of the greatest to me, that is of having made up my good resolutions for the future; that the Retreat may not pass without leaving some good impressions in my mind."

Sunday, March 25.

"This morning I received the *Alameda Gazette*. I saw in the Gazette that Mr. Ward would be in court involved in many cases of the Ranch, at least six, I saw in the Court calendar. . . . This evening it commenced raining at nine o'clock and gave the appearance of long duration. I have at present a terrible sore throat, but do not go to the Infirmary as yet."

On the following morning J.M awakened with a severe headache, plus an inflamed throat. Several students were already in the infirmary with similar ailments which was of great concern to the Fathers because there had been several cases of typhoid fever in Santa Clara. Chilling winds and heavy rains again came to the valley and a fresh, light blanket of snow lay on the highest peaks. Four days later, a heavy hail storm stripped the orchards of all blooms and flattened great patches of wild flowers on the lowlands. J.M. continued his studies with feverish eyes, and huddled close to the little, wood-burning stove in the study hall. The month of March had entered as the proverbial lamb and departed like a charging lion.

7

April and May

The first three days of April were depressingly dreary. J.M. thought the sun would never shine again, but on the fourth, he wrote: "Today we may say Glory Alleluliah [*sic*] for the beautiful day we had. This morning they commenced to bring bricks for the new building. After dinner the cadets assembled in the Reading Room, and a contribution of fifty cents from each cadet was raised to pay the expenses of the Captain [Robert Keating] to San Francisco, in order to procure rifles. F. Messea gave us today an analysis of the silver ores and we had to write a lecture upon the analysis of the silver ores of Washoe. Whilst in the laboratory F. Messea told me that I have taken a good view of the subject in the last lecture, but that I did not bring any experiments."

Sunday, April 6.

"This morning before study, Roche and myself went into a room to write our compositions. This afternoon we had catechism as usual after which I went to take a walk with Father Nattini. B. Murphy and Bowie also went. We stopped to see the graveyards, Protestant and Catholic, we took a long walk and came in just in time for supper."

April 8.

"After chemistry class, while I was in the study room, I felt very bad, a terrible headache that I could not finish my French exercise and after study I went to the Infirmary and laid on a bed. Seeing that it did me little good, I determined to remain in the Infirmary for the evening. I took a foot bath and then covered myself well in order to prespire [*sic*]. This evening it rained a good deal."

Epidemics of this type had felled Californios since the earliest days of colonization. Deaths attributed to this ailment were recorded at Monterey in 1806 about four or five months after Jose Maria Estudillo's wife had had their second child at the post. J.M. remained in the infirmary through the following day, but was well enough to read *The Perfect Gentlemen*. On April 10, he returned to his classes and later joined his friends who were flying kites in the recreational area. To their delight, they noted two young ladies watching them from the windows of an adobe home across the roadway.

Sunday, April 13.

"Holy Week begins today, this morning we received in church, palms, olive branches, as today is Palm Sunday. Heard this afternoon of the great fight at Pittsburgh Landing. Keating came to the college today, and he tried his best to get an act passed in the Legislature to provide the colleges with arms, as that fifty-eight had already been reported."

The Battle of Shiloh, Tennessee, or "Pittsburgh Landing" began at dawn on April 6, and lasted for two days. The conflict was one of the most furious of the Civil War. More than ten thousand Confederates were killed or wounded and nearly twelve thousand of their greatly outnumbered enemy [John Laird Wilson, *Pictorial History of the Great Civil War*]. W.H. Brewer wrote that when the news arrived in San Francisco at ten o'clock the night of April 12, the city was in great excitement. "People were out, at midnight a salute of cannon was fired, and the streets were noisy all night long as if it had been the Fourth of July." The excitement continued throughout the following day. Brewer added: "T. Starr King delivered a patriotic sermon that night, the anniversary of the fall of Fort Sumter, which, although probably hardly appropriate for Sunday, was nevertheless a most brilliant and eloquent performance."

April 14.

"I saw in the 'Alta' that a bill had passed for granting arms to Colleges and academies and this will be good for us." Three days later he added:

April 17.

"This has been a warm day. This morning we did not hear Mass in the chapel, went to the big church [the fifth chapel of Mission Santa Clara] at half past nine and heard high Mass, many people went to communion. During a conversation with Father Accolti [Professor of Divinity, General Jurisprudence and Science of Government], I learnt how Mr. Judah became bankrupt. By the wharf he undertook to make at Redwood City and that he lost all the property, [and] land he had for bad title.

In 1853, the remunerative lumber industry in San Mateo County prompted many to invest in mills and properties. A few, including Mr. Charles Judah, purchased a sizable tract of land fronting the ocean to establish a lumber-shipping town named *Ravenswood.* However, after a few years, the venture proved to be a great disappointment. The shipping point was abandoned and the great, redwood wharf was left to rot and ultimately broke apart. [*History of San Mateo County, California,* B.F. Alley, Publisher, p. 229.] Mr. Judah's investments became a complete loss. His financial status rose again when he and Mr. John Nugent established a law firm in San Francisco.

I also learnt that Mr. Judah had always professed to be a Catholic. Of this I only knew that he had a good religious principle, as I heard the Archbishop Alemany once in the city express the same sentiments. After some time he (Father Accolti) asked me if Mr. John Nugent was a good Catholic now. I answered in the affirmative and said there was a time when nobody knew what he was. This conversation took place in the Fathers' yard. . . ."

The students usually worshipped in the small, but attractive Gothic brick chapel, constructed under the supervision of Father John Nobili, S.J. in the early 1850s. It stood at a short distance from the Mission Church, the main entrance faced the Alameda to the north. The main entrance of the students' chapel faced West and was so designed by Father Nobili, S.J. to keep students from being distracted by young ladies from Santa Clara and San Jose upon entering or leaving the main house of worship.

April 18.
"Good Friday. We went to church just the same as yesterday, but remained a longer time. We kissed the crucifix. I put twenty-five cents in the plate. I hurt my thumb whilst playing the Flying Dutchman, almost out of joint. After supper we were allowed to go to the washroom and get ready for the procession. I carried the picture of the Blessed Virgin; Bowie, the crucifix, assisted by Palmer and Duffy, and I, by D. Delmas and Sposito. We went through all the passion of our Lord, stopping at all

the stations in the church, came to the chapel (students') and Father Prelatto preached a short sermon, then we went to study."

Good Friday, April 19, 1864.

"In Spanish countries on this day, no one is allowed to ride a horse or drive unless it is indispensable to do so."

Sunday, April 20.

"Easter Sunday. Went to communion. Father Villiger [Father Burchard Villiger, S.J.] said Mass and preached a very interesting sermon. We had quite a good breakfast, nothing very extra. I had twenty eggs after breakfast and played with the other boys at cracking. The dinner was pretty good. Among the desserts there was my favorite dish, the floating islands. At half past two, we went out walking on the San Jose Road, went almost to the bridge, came back a little after supper. I was very tired."

The custom of egg-cracking was brought from Spain and Mexico by the early Californios and practiced on Easter Sunday, Christmas, at weddings, and other festive occasions, but never in public. After a small hole had been made at each end of a raw egg, the contents were blown out. One end was then sealed with wax. After water, cologne, tinsel, or tiny bits of colored paper had been inserted from the opposite end, the opening was carefully sealed. These were known as "Cascarones" and were to be broken upon the head of an unsuspecting person, however, it was considered improper to break more than one egg at a time. R.N. Dana, Jr. witnessed a "cracking" in Santa Barbara in 1835 and noted that several of the ladies kept cologne-filled eggs hidden about their person until they found a suitable victim. When an egg was broken upon the head of a gentleman, he, in gallantry, was obliged to seek the lady and return the compliment, but only in surprise. [Dana, Jr., *op cit,* p. 158, 1840 edition.]

A notation in the back of *Journal for 1862* states that J.M. paid twenty-five cents for the twenty eggs which he probably purchased from the farmer who sold eggs and milk to housewives in the vicinity of the college. The usual method of selling milk was quite simple. The farmer merely led his cow by a rope from one dwelling to another where it was milked when the housewife provided the necessary container. The charge depended upon the size of the container.

April 21.

". . . Father Caredda this morning reminded us of a few points in the rules of the College and during the forenoon the principal rules of the College were hung in the windows of the study room." [Some of Father Caredda's disciplinary measures appear in J.M. Estudillo's *Journal for 1864.*] "After he had read the written rules, he said that there were four or five different spirits in the College but how they came in, he did not know—viz, Spirit of Novel Reading, 2nd, Spirit of Gambling, 3rd, Spirit of Laziness, 4th, Spirit of Destruction, by which different kinds of furniture had been spoiled, such as doors, and desks disfigured in the like manner."

In the same journal, the diarist wrote that Thomas Van Ness was expelled because he had mailed several personal letters "through the wrong channels." He had been warned against this several times. All letters were to be mailed from the president's office where each envelope was closely examined before it was permitted to leave the institution for mailing. Six days after Van Ness' departure, Napoleon Donavan was expelled for the same offense.

"Aug. Spivalo was here this afternoon and says that we might get the rifles in about a month. Last night I was pretty sick. I passed a very bad night, slept very little. I studied my grammar and read a few pages of the Life of Curran, by his son."

April 22.

"Received this afternoon the Alameda [County] Gazette and see by last week's news of San Leandro, that preparations are being made for the execution of Bonny, a scaffold is in construction in the rear of the Court House."

At the session of the District Court held in March, 1861, E.W. Bonny of San Leandro, was indicted for the murder of his friend, Auguste Hirsche and was subsequently convicted of the crime. Although Bonny protested his innocence, the verdict against him was most conclusive. On July 27, 1861, the Grand Jury found Bonny guilty in the first degree. J.M. attended the trial because Bonny was well known to the Estudillo family and later wrote that the unfortunate man's ". . . mother felt very bad, but his father was very cool."

April 25.

"During the hours of ten and twelve this morning, I have thought a good deal of Bonny whose execution was to take place between the hours of ten and twelve. Do not know yet if the execution has taken place. James Whitney was here this afternoon. He looks very thin, has been on the point of dying, has come for his health." [James and his brothers Abbott L. and William of San Francisco were boarding Students of Santa Clara College.] "Nothing else transpired today."

April 26.
". . . This afternoon we had a composition in Natural Philosophy, to describe the Electric Machine and the Leyden Jar. Father Caredda gave me my Bulletin, I sent it this evening to Mr. Ward. I had in Conduct—good; Improvement—Fast Enough; Application—Great; Health—Good, of course no bad notes."

April 28.
"Received this afternoon the [Sacramento] *Union* and the *Alameda Gazette*. I saw in the *Gazette* that the Hotel (Estudillo House) had been leased by W.K. Stokes and Imerman. I saw that Bonny had been hung at the time his execution was to take place. In philosophy class the boys were not very gentlemanly, like in the cabinet and so F. Masnata made us come to the class room." [On the following day, J.M. received a letter informing him that his brother, Jose Antonio, had again left for the Washoe Silver Mines.]

April 30.
"This afternoon we did not have the monthly places as we expected; for the reasons I believe of being too much occupied with the drama. As soon as we were out of class, we got into the washroom and prepared ourselves for the Drama Entertainment. At seven P.M. we came to the theater, I was appointed by Father Young to be usher for the evening, so was James Breen. We did not have a very large crowd, but I believe they made about one hundred and fifty dollars. The pieces played were the following: The 'Merchant of Venice,' 'The Specter Bridegroom,' a farce in one act and 'The Wandering Minstrel,' a farce in one act. Everything was over at quarter past eleven."

May 1.
"Splendid time! Picnic, picnic!!! I got permission to go out, and soon did I put my desires into execution. I got to San Jose about ten o'clock

A.M. and then I met Palmer, Keating and Murphy. Palmer and myself got ready to go to the Burnett's picnic. I was invited by Prevost. Palmer drove the horse and buggy, after an hour and a half of traveling we came to the desired spot; but nevertheless, had to make a small mistake, we expected the picnic was at the house of Mr. Burnett, not so, it was two miles further on Stevens' Creek. After a hard travel we got to the desired spot. For a picturesque scene, this spot can hardly be surpassed. Here indeed the work of Nature has displayed its wondrous hand in the land-scape of the country around the spot of the pleasure enjoyment. Flowery green meadows with a beautiful running stream was a sight for a poet to contemplate upon. The fair sex, among whom there were many hand-some ones, seemed to enjoy themselves under the shade of an alder tree whose branches covered us from the sun. I did not partake in the dance. My acquaintances were, I mean in the female line, were Miss Sunol, Miss Bascom, to the latter I did not speak. Of course, Lizzie Miller was there. We had plenty of champagne, cakes and everything we could wish. Soon after we left on our way home, but we could not find the right road; but after Bernard Murphy took the lead and we found our-selves in Santa Clara. I saw at Cameron's Hotel some of the Hoges family. [Cameron's Hotel, the *Mansion House,* stood on the corner of Franklin and Lafayette Streets in Santa Clara. It had been the *Union Hotel,* built by a Captain Anson in 1850, until it was purchased seven years later by Mr. W.M. Cameron.] The afternoon after we got to Santa Clara was very windy and during the whole of the night the wind blew extremely hard. It was a little too warm when we left San Jose, but as soon as we got to the mountains a few drops of rain fell but did not continue."

J.M. probably avoided Miss Bascom because she was a Methodist, a faith he deemed especially intolerable. J.M. was first introduced to Miss Bascom at a picnic in 1861. This charming and well-educated young lady was a younger daughter of Dr. and Mrs. L.H. Bascom who arrived in California in 1849 and about two years later settled in Santa Clara. Their daughter, Henrianna, married Captain W.F. Swasey, the noted pioneer and author of *The Days and Men of California,* published in 1891. By 1860, Captain and Mrs. Swasey were living in a two-story, Victorian home on the corner of Bush and Mason Streets in San Fran-cisco.

On May 5, the day after one of the students died of consumption J.M. wrote:

"This day shall never be blotted out of the tablets of my memory, a thing happened today which shall remain in character of indelible ink before my eyes, and this is the funeral of Henry O'Toole, a student, who a year ago conversed with me within this College, now is no more. An impression has been made on me that I could not but retain my tears when his lifeless corpse was lowered into the grave. The funeral procession was arranged in the following manner. Ahead of all was the Cadet's Band, next the cadets, in two platoons, and then the hearse was next. Behind the hearse followed the smaller boys and the parents, etc. The band played when going as when coming. I had forgotten to say that Mass was said for the repose of the soul of the deceased. Before the corpse had been taken away from the Church, Father Young made a few remarks to the congregation and inspired them to continue in virtue, at the same time making known the virtues of Henry O'Toole when in College. A Sodalist, and example to all of his companions in the frequent approach to the Sacraments, he was not ashamed to practice his religion before his companions. Not to weep for him but to weep for ourselves and remember that sooner or later we shall all follow the same road. Today it shall be remembered that the new building commenced, things got ready, such as the carpenters' shop, measured the ground, etc."

May 6.

"After dinner the cadets elected Thomas Van Ness as Fourth Sergeant. During the chemistry class, our professor employed the hour of the class speaking more about political matters than on platinum, spoke about the approaching war that would be in the whole of Europe, then of iron-clad vessels, etc., etc. The building is progressing very fast, the lumber commenced to be hauled today."

The professors probably spoke of the battle that took place on March 9, 1862, between the iron-clad vessels, the "Monitor" and the "Merrimac" at Hampton Roads which caused controversial opinions throughout the country respecting the value of defense.

May 8.

"Anniversary of the cadets. After many preparations and expectations, at last the day arrived when we expect to show the people of San Jose what we can do. After marching through Santa Clara we started for San Jose for which I contributed fifty cents. At the first bridge [Los Gatos Creek], we stopped and fell into ranges. In passing through the town the citizens seemed quite astonished at the marshalled appearance of the cadets. After making a short rest at the hotel [Crandell's] we assembled at the table to do honor to the occasion, in partaking of a sumptuous collation, to which great zest was added by complimentary toasts. Lunch being over, we proceeded to the garden of Prevost where we were to have target excursion. After taking arms we walked to the places where the target was placed, the distance measured, seventy-five yards, with rifles. The first shot was fired by Lieut. Murphy, or I believe the Captain, but the Captain did not hit the target. Murphy's shot struck the target, but far from the bull's eye. The shooting continued from the first platoon down, few of any consequence, the most missed the target entirely. I shall not be proud of having the honor of the day. I hit the bull's eye an inch from the middle. James Whitney made the next best shot. Hastings, at fifty yards, made the best shot of all. I received the badge and Valenzuela received the leader medal. Many persons were at the spot to see us shoot, as well as ladies. Soon after we came home, marched a good deal through town, but still more in front of the Convent, the band played two tunes, the windows were crowded with convent girls. Arrived at the College at almost dark, for we marched once more through Santa Clara. Had Holy night at supper. Sposito made a speech and stood upon one of the tables, he was perfectly enraged at the boys because they laughed at him. I was exceedingly tired and was glad to get to bed when the time came."

Sunday, May 11.

"Today we honor St. Joseph for its being a patron day of such a great saint, we kept it much a holy day, for we had no study or catechism. I finished reading 'Adam, The Grizzly Bear Hunter of California.'" [Theodore H. Hittell's well-known book, *Adventures of James Adams— Mountaineer and Grizzly Bear Hunter of California* was published in 1860.]

May 12.

"I saw in the *Gazette* that the execution of Edward W. Bonny took place last Friday, May 9, at San Leandro. It was the first Legal execution held in Alameda County [W. Halley, *op cit* p. 163]. I saw in the *Union* that Jose Maria [Estudillo, his cousin in San Diego] had been appointed Notary Public for the County of San Diego." [Jose Maria Estudillo of San Diego was named in honor of his paternal grandfather, the founder of

California's Estudillo families. Young Jose Maria was born in 1830, baptized at Mission San Diego de Alcala. On July 1, 1862, married Luz Marron. (Biographical files, *Estudillo,* San Diego Historical Society.)]

"This afternoon there were some outside visitors, John M. Burnett, Mr. Thompson with Lizzie Miller and three or four young ladies. I took quite an exercise digging in the foundation of the new building which is progressing very fast. Weather cold and a few drops of rain this afternoon, but it seems to continue."

May 15.

"We had speaking class, I spoke Durand's 'Union Forever.' F. Young made me repeat the first stanza two or three times and I got a little confused and displeased and so came down from the stage wishing almost never to speak another speech, but soon my passions were calmed and proposed to speak well next Friday. Tonight at the Office of the Month of Mary, the meditation was on the glory of heaven. As Father Aloysius Masnata read, his face wore a smiling countenance as he read the beautiful description of the heavenly choirs, etc."

May 17.

"This evening I went to confession, and have resolved to continue the following for Saturdays and of course ot communion. A new book was commenced reading in the refectory, finished the life of Daniel Boone. . . . I got today, my three lectures made in chemistry, viz, some experiments on gasses, 2nd., artificial light; 3rd, analysis of Washoe silver ore. Today we were told not to go near the foundation of the building, much less to interfere with the workmen."

May 18.

"I went out walking with some boys and Father Nattini, walked as far as the first bridge and then came home. . . . After supper I spoke to Breen to write me a speech for the exhibition and he very kindly proposed to do it. Palmer this evening was caught making a cigarrito in the Refectory and Father Caredda has given him a punishment, but Palmer would not submit and proposes to leave the College tomorrow."

The decision to leave the college was not Palmer's. Students who refused punishment were expelled after their parents or guardians were first notified and given full details of the misbehavior.

May 19.

"It is sad to record, that a friend, whose friendship I always kept sealed with the truest bond of affection, was turned out of the College last night, he was not even permitted to pass the night at the College. Father Caredda spoke to us in the Refectory and for many other reasons, better known to them (the faculty), Edward Palmer was expelled after dinner. I heard Palmer had been in the College last night but did not see him. . . ."

May 23.

"Tonight we went to the circus, F. Mengarini went for the first time in his life. We were all pleased with the performance, especially with the gymnastics of the three little boys. There was a great crowd. The bearded lady and the man that swallows stones were there. At half past ten the show was over and soon we made our way home, after a short prayer in the chapel went to bed."

Sunday, May 25.

"After catechism class, Breen gave me the speech he had promised to write for me; 'The Storming of Quebec—1776,' and a very long piece of one-hundred and seventy-three lines. I did not go walking on account of having to stop and commence learning it. I learnt [*sic*] sixteen lines, not very well, but enough for the time I had. This evening's study I had a terrible headache and it was caused by my studying so hard this afternoon and this evening I had to study about twenty pages of history."

On the following morning, J.M. was very depressed, fatigued and worried. For some unknown reason, his friend, Thomas Duffy asked for a copy of "The Storming of Quebec." The request irritated J.M. considerably, but it was granted. His worries and self-pity mounted by the hour, especially after reading in the *Gazette* that a great ball was to take place at the "Estudillo House" which he would be unable to attend.

May 28.

"It is sad to record, but yet it cannot be helped, that today we laid the remains of the lamented Armsted Burnett to his last resting place. He died on Monday night. The funeral procession was quite large and the cadets accompanied the hearse with the old muskets. The band played the same tunes that they played at O'Toole's funeral. All the beauty of San Jose was there though with weeping eyes, their faces smiling as ever."

Armsted was a son of the Honorable Peter H. Burnett; he had received his S.B. Degree from Santa Clara College in 1859.

May 31.

"Father Nattini told the boys in public in the study room, that the private examinations would begin on the tenth of next month. Whilst I write these few lines I cannot but feel glad to say that I passed that month of May as a Christian ought to. . . ."

8

The Close of the Spring Semester

Sunday, June 1.

"Went to communion. This morning Mr. John O'Dougherty came to visit me and I showed him around the college with Father Neri, he was very much pleased with the college and promised to come for the exhibition (the closing exercises). We had composition in catechism, but not in what I expected; nevertheless, I made a pretty good one. After catechism I went swimming with the boys; this is my first time this session and may be the last for it did not make a very good impression; I got a headache by going in the water. James Breen went away today; he passed an examination and will get the degree S.B. He left on account of his health. . . ."

The swimming pool on the campus, fed by an artesian well, was 160 by 120 feet. However, the boys often preferred Guadalupe creek about one and one half miles from the college. Here they could swing from the willows, catch frogs, chase ducks and be more boisterous and relaxed in their deportment. J.M.'s headache continued through the following day which he attributed to ". . . being overwhelmed with lessons to prepare for the coming week." On June 3, John Roche was sent home because of illness and although the diarist was still indisposed, he forced himself to memorize the speech he was to deliver at the closing exercises.

June 6.

"Father Nattini asked me for the names of the officers of the Debating Society and I gave them to him; as for Vice-President, Cunningham; we had a meeting and expelled him for sending the Society to use some expression like his "to the warm regions below" and for other sundry things; he was not present at the meeting. Mr. Townsend was elected in Mr. Cunningham's place."

The Philatelic Debating Society was organized on February 22, 1857. The officers for the first two years were: Rev. Michael Accolti, S.J., Moderator; Master W. Rowe, Vice-President; Master Frank Bray, Treasurer; Master John Bray, Secretary; and Master John Burnett, Censor.

June 8.

"This morning I went to communion. The Very Rev. Bishop Amat of Monterey officiated. The Mass was longer than usual. Great indeed must have been the joy of John Burnett, as well as all of his relatives as it was ours to have had today the happiness of entering the fold of the Holy Catholic Church. The baptismal ceremony took place in the large church. All the boys that wished to attend were present. I of course was there. Martin Murphy [Junior] was his god-father and his godmother, I do not know who she was. We had quite a good dinner, being a great feast day, Pentecost. Of course we had not catechism and this afternoon I went walking towards San Jose. Today it blew all day."

June 9.

"The private examinations began today, they commenced with all the small boys in the preparatory Dept. Received this afternoon a letter from Dolores and the papers; I see by Dolores' letter that Magdalena [his sister, Mrs. John Nugent] has brought forth a child, a girl named Sybil, and she is well. This evening during the first hour of study I and Marks and Duffy were in Father Caredda's room to write the invitations for the exhibition. . . . I gave Father Caredda the name of my speech of the exhibition, to be put in the programme, he told me that he would not promise to call me as there were so many speeches already. . . ."

June 10.

"Today I was very much displeased in the way Father Young treated me concerning my speech after having given it to him two weeks ago, he comes now, that there is no time to speak it in the exhibition, yes, for me there is no time, but for the rest, there is plenty. In chemistry class the compositions were brought in, but I promised Father Messea to give him mine this evening, but I did not on account of having gone to the exhibition of the other college and coming home so late. Seven of us boys went with Father Young. If at our exhibitions, we could not do better I would duck my head. The most ridiculous speaking I have ever heard, for example; 'Policy of the Administration' and two others. I saw Miss Hall and five girls of the Seminary sat right behind us and with their fan, they gave me and James Hughes more than the air needed."

Miss Bascom was a devout Methodist. As a child of the Spanish civilization, J.M. inherited the memory of long rivalry, religious and political differences between England and Spain. From early childhood, he overheard lengthy discussions pertaining to this country's acquisition of Texas, New Mexico, and California. He witnessed the encroachment of squatters on Rancho San Leandro and El Rancho Pinole and may have blamed their decline upon the squatters and cattle rustlers, most of whom he presumed were not of his faith. It is likely that he identified all Protestants with the "Yankee" settlers and lawyers whom he blamed for his mother's financial difficulties.

Upon his return from the program given by the literary society of the Methodist College of the Pacific in 1864, he wrote: "The exercises of the evening were four or five speeches, music by their miserable band and prayer by their President." In the same year, after reading of Reverend Thomas Starr King's death on March 4, 1864 and the lengthy tributes paid him by innumerable citizens and periodicals, J.M. again vented his emotions by writing: "Poor Fellow, I pity him, a man eloquent undoubtedly, but with what principle." At one time, he referred to the Masonic Order as "that accursed society." Could he have known of the tremendous work and contributions the order made to aid the countless unfortunates during the gold rush and the floods of 1861-1862, and still have written so unjustly? Weeks before the diarist's sister, Dolores, was to marry Mr. Charles H. Cushing, a cultured Protestant from Boston, J.M. lay awake night after night in worry, disapproval, and bitter disappointment. That his favorite sister was to marry a "Yankee" protestant was beyond his comprehension. After the wedding reception on August 14, 1864, the bridal couple left for Warm Springs. That evening, he wrote: "I did not care to see the bride and groom leave for the Springs, for I knew what my feelings would be at that time. . . ."

June 19.

"Received this afternoon a letter from Mr. Ward where he tells me that he intends to be present at the exhibition and has invited Mr. Nugent to accompany him. I hope nothing may occur to detain them. I heard that

Lola is pretty sick and they are waiting till the exhibition is over so that I can accompany her to a trip to Los Angeles. This forenoon the two debating societies went to the other college at Cook's Grove, quite a number of people were present. Nothing was done worth praising, and the ridiculous thing of introducing the speakers to the public in Latin was done by the President. Dr. Peck delivered an address with two of the graduates. . . ."

June 17.

"At half past four or thereabouts, I rehearsed my speech in the theater before Father Young and his remarks were that I did not know it as well as he expected. I said nothing, but within me I felt the kind of a madness to see with what scorn he talked to me."

Undoubtedly the diarist's inferiority complex was accentuated in the presence of Father Young who did not appreciate J.M.'s emotional and sensitive nature. A notation in J.M.'s *Journal for 1864* attests that Father Neri was more understanding. It reads: "Oh! Neri, Neri, blessings be upon thy head for casting a few beams of bright sunlight upon this otherwise dry pathway of life." Occasionally J.M.'s emotions were almost beyond control. After a church service in the same year, he wrote: ". . . The pathetic part was very affecting; but because I had a small handkerchief, I could not begin to cry for fear that I would not have another dry enough to dry my tears."

June 19.

"Corpus Christi. This morning being a great feast day, it was celebrated with High Mass and a procession was as follows: Head of all was the Cross, and next came the small girls [from the Convent of Notre Dame] with their ensign, which looked admirably well. Next followed the boys of the Sodality. I was marshall of the right and Delmas of the left. Next was the band followed by the Blessed Sacrament and the cadets followed. We had quite a good dinner. We had not studied during the whole day and this evening only a very short time, because we came from seeing the railroad tracks at a rather late hour. Some time after dinner I went into one of the class rooms with Van Ness to recite my speech, quite a warm day."

June 23.

"School ceased today, we packed our trunks during the forenoon. I went swimming in the afternoon. After we had finished packing, some eight or ten boys, I among them, were engaged in fixing the theater scenes. After this work we had a treat of wine and cakes for a recompense of our work. This evening we had a rehearsal of the drama, went to bed at half past nine."

June 24.

"We expected to have slept more than usual, but no, we were aroused at the usual hour. At half past ten I went to San Jose, took Manuel Torres and James Smith with me. I went to see the exhibition of the young ladies [Convent of Notre Dame] took lunch with Schaffner. I saw Mr. Curtis also Manuel Torres and Manuelita.

"I remained in San Jose till Mr. Ward and my mother came in the Oakland stage, we went together to Santa Clara. Our exhibition commenced this evening. There was a large crowd. I was usher of the evening. After everything was over I went out with Mr. Ward and took a buggy at Cameron's Hotel and drove to San Jose. This was about twelve o'clock. All the hotels were full at San Jose. Slept in an old house. John Murphy was with us."

The "exhibition" was the first of the Eleventh Annual Commencement Exercises at Santa Clara College. Among those on the program were Thomas Duffy, whose subject was "Home." Marshall Hastings spoke on "Artificial Light" and John Townsend with Thomas Marks, presented a dialogue entitled "The Professions." The two most outstanding presentations were a discourse given by Michael Delmas and a debate: "Is Man Endowed with a Free Will," presented by Bernard Daniel Murphy and Robert Keating.

The second part of the exercises took place on the following afternoon, when J.M. delivered his "Storming of Quebec." The program included a few short addresses and a tune presented by the college band. This was followed by Augustus J. Bowie's piano rendition of "Prayer From Othello" and a few other classical numbers. Saturnino Ayon of Mexico, Thomas Marks, and Marshall A. Shaffner also played piano solos which were followed by skilled violin solos presented by Thomas Duffy. The college band closed the afternoon program with "Home Sweet Home."

J.M. wrote: "After the first tune of the band, I opened the program by a speech 'Storming of Quebec.' This I take notice for being my first speech in public. The exercises of the day were crowdedly attended, but to say nothing of the drama and distributions of premiums, they were immensely crowded. The drama came off very well, 'The Merchant of Venice' . . . The degree of A.B. was conferred on M. Delmas, and S.B. on Breen, Keating and Murphy. After the conferring of degrees, the premiums were given. I was equal in conduct with Delmas. I got the medal. I also was first in Catechism and in Neatness and Politeness and also was first, alone. I got the second premium in Geography and would have got the first if the other boy had not in the premium-composition copied from the Atlas—this was Ayon (of Mexico). After everything was over I went and told good-bye to some of the Fathers. We came to San Jose that evening, which was about twelve or still later. Slept at Crandell's hotel—many of the boys were there. I saw Miss Shaffner with Manuelita Smith."

June 26.

"Got up very early for the Oakland stage. Started from San Jose at half past five a.m. and got to San Leandro at half past eleven. I had quite a pleasant trip, sat with the driver. After dinner I went to Vicente's house, I went out shooting for a short time, I killed three doves. I helped Vicente to kill a young heifer and after we had finished Vicente went to the corral and when there, one of his Indian boys, John, was badly injured by a raged bull. He received a wound in the thigh and this evening I could not sleep on account of his groans, but worst of all, the bull itself came to the house and began to bellow till Vicente shot him with a gun and Federico, another Indian vaquero, drove him away on horseback."

Friday, June 27.

"Got up very early and came to San Leandro, brought the sick boy in a wagon, left him at the 'Emperor's.' After breakfast I took Mr. Ward's buggy and drove to Vicente's house to get a riding saddle. I got one at half past ten A.M. I started for San Joaquin, stopped at Mr. Tennent's, had lunch. I am sorry to say I was forced to eat meat. The day was very warm. I got to San Joaquin in the afternoon. I gave a prospectus to John O'Neil. At six, I took a short ride to see Jose Antonio [Martinez'] orchard and fetched a horse to bring to San Leandro but it happened not to be the right one. I saw there Jose Ramon, Luis and Frank Ward."

June 29, 1864.

"This is my birthday, and tonight at ten o'clock I am twenty years old. Twenty summers have passed over this head, and oh, how shall I look to this past time, could I regret it, or am I glad that it has passed never to come back? This evening we drank some champagne in the parlor. I began to read the 'Waverly' novels. Nothing of particular notice transpired."

9

July

July 1.

"I got up at a very late hour, took a bath and went for a walk and visited some friends. According to promise I went to see Miss Hart and we came in the omnibus to see Magdalena. I went out at half past four, went to see Calvin and also made young Mr. Phelan's acquaintance. Came home, took dinner and went to the steroptican views, remained till everything was over then came home and went to bed."

Two days later, J.M. ordered a tailor-made suit at Mr. James Tobin's establishment located at 619 Montgomery Street. San Francisco was busy preparing for the 4th of July. Countless flags already waved throughout the business district while great lengths of bunting were being draped along the main thoroughfares. Livery stables were busy grooming horses, polishing and decorating carriages and wagons that were to carry various bands and the city's notables. Because great throngs were to enjoy the celebration, J.M. hoped he would meet many of his college associates and not be obliged to wander about alone.

July 4.

"This day was handsomely celebrated at San Francisco; a large procession paraded through the principal streets. I saw it pass through Montgomery. I was with George Hoge at his father's office, we went together to take some ice cream. . . . The fireworks were very fine, I went to bed very early, eleven. I say early because it being the Fourth of July most probably I would have remained later, I was rather lonesome.

"Would to God that the peace that once reigned over this land return.

82

In what unison we would celebrate this immortal day. But whether North or South, this is a day which no party spirit should influence us to celebrate in a manner worthy of it. Why should a Jeff Davis sympathizer, refuse to do justice—today I say, sound the loud trumpet, let cheerfulness be shown. I, who though not a free born American, feel a little of that spirit which raises, and makes every American's heart leap with gladness at the very name of Liberty, what then must be the feeling of a United Nation when paying honor to the Fourth of July."

In San Leandro hundreds celebrated the 4th at the Estudillo House. Picnics and festivities were held all along the upper course of San Leandro Creek. In nearby Hayward, over a thousand people attended a great "Union" meeting and later watched a procession of gaily-decorated conveyances of varied types and sizes, parade through the settlement and thence through San Lorenzo and San Leandro. This celebration closed with a ball at Hayward's Hotel, where dancing and musical numbers lasted far beyond midnight. By that time, J.M. was already deep in slumber.

On the following day, loneliness prompted him to attend confession at St. Ignatius Church and visit briefly with the Fathers. In the afternoon he again called upon Miss Hart ". . . but my usual luck, she was not at home." On Sunday, July 6, he attended Mass at Oakland's St. Mary's Church and later continued to ride about in search of companionship. Towards evening, he decided to visit his sister, Lola, but this proved to be a bitter disappointment. Lola was entertaining Miss Gettin, and after playing a few games of cards with them, the young ladies resorted to teasing J.M. by insisting that he dress as a woman. Because it disgusted and embarrassed him, he left the young ladies without bidding them good evening and hurriedly walked to the Estudillo House where he was boarding.

July 7.
"Came to the city, I drove Mr. Ward's mare. Lola and Eulalia (Vicente Estudillo's wife) came with me. I got some little things for my trip to Los Angeles, such as shirts, etc. I went to see Calvin and congratulated him on his married state. I went to see Palmer at his cousin's office. Today I ordered a pair of boots to be made."

July 10.
"I wrote a letter to Sophia [Ward] at Benicia. This morning and all

afternoon I passed in the house but at one o'clock I took a ride as far as Oakland, but my intention was to go to San Joaquin, but I met the 'Emperor' and left him go and came back. I took Mr. Ward's mare to the ranch [San Leandro]. Raphael Peralta and myself came together. We rode very slow. After supper we took a walk in the garden, Miss Gettin and Lola accompanying."

In the Victorian era, it was deemed improper for a well-bred, unmarried young couple to wander about unchaperoned, especially after dark. In 1867, after a dinner party at the Estudillos' home, Mrs. John Nugent and Juana Estudillo chanced to see J.M. and a young lady enjoying a beautiful evening in the garden for which he was later severely reprimanded by his mother. He later wrote: "I must say that I retired in a bad humor."

On July 13, J.M. dined with the Wards and Nugents and played with little Johnnie or John Francis, the son of Mr. and Mrs. John B. Ward.

The child's twin brother had died shortly after birth in 1859. [Personal interview with Miss Evelyn Ward, granddaughter of John B. Ward.] After breakfast on the following morning, J.M. went shopping in anticipation of a journey to Los Angeles. "I took my new pair of boots and then went to see my black suit which was being made at Mr. Tobin's, it was not ready yet. Came to Blums and got a light gray suit and then went to the Metropolitan Hotel to see Marshall Shaffner but he was not at home, after this I went home."

In the afternoon of July 15, he again went to the Metropolitan Hotel where he spoke briefly to Mr. Abel Stearns, a prominent Californian and intimate friend of William Heath Davis and both branches of the Estudillo families. Mr. Abel Stearns was a native of Massachusetts and known to the early Californians as *Don Abel*. In 1833, shortly after his arrival in Los Angeles, Mr. Stearns became a Mexican citizen and entered a trading partnership with Don Juan Bandini. During the ensuing years, Mr. Stearns acquired great wealth and vast acreage. He became one of the largest land-owners in Southern California [*Sheldon G. Jackson, A British Ranchero:* Henry Dalton, p. 62]. Most notable of his holdings was his *Rancho Los Alamitos* and his sprawling, adobe home in Los Angeles, constructed for his wife, Arcadia, a daughter of Don Juan Bandini. In 1849, Mr. Stearns was a member of the delegation to the *Constitutional Convention* held in Monterey.

J.M. then called for his black suit and returned to the Nugents' home where he ". . . learned from Mr. Ward that it was decided to delay our trip to Los Angeles till the next steamer."

Mr. Ward had already left the Nugents by the time J.M. awakened on the following morning, but ". . . I went and got a horse and buggy and took a drive about town, went to South Park, took Palmer with me, came back and put her in the stable." Sometime later he and Ward rode in a carriage to the Hibernia Society and endorsed notes to the amount of two thousand and four hundred dollars.

Mr. Ward kept his horse and carriage at Gough's Livery Stable in San Francisco, but when J.M. needed a carriage in Oakland, he was obliged to hire one for $3.00 at the Shattuck and Hillegas Livery Stable on the east side of Broadway, between Front and Fifth Streets.

July 17.

"I was up this morning a little earlier than usual. Soon got ready to go to the city on the way to Benicia, passed to the city on the second boat with Mrs. Ward [his sister, Concepcion], my mother and Mr. Ward, also Johnnie. In the city I was to visit Mrs. Stearns and soon left for Benicia, on the 'New World,' Mrs. Ward, my mother in company."

Thomas O. Larkin, a very successful merchant and probably the most prominent American in Alta California (*Sheldon G. Jackson, A British Ranchero,* Henry Dalton, p. 63), Dr. Robert Semple, General M.G. Vallejo and their associates believed that Benicia would become the greatest city in California, but the geographical location of San Francisco and its rapid progress soon over-shadowed the development of Benicia. The settlement fronted about three miles of the *Suisun,* the upper division of San Francisco Bay.

"I enjoyed the trip very much but my mother and Mrs. Ward were seasick part of the way, arrived at Benicia about a quarter to seven, took a stage and went to the Convent, saw Sophia [Ward] and remained quite a lengthy time there, came to the hotel and engaged rooms, I was very unlucky, I had a very bad room. Mr. Sweeney [Miles D. Sweeny of San Francisco] was with us part of the time."

After William H. Brewer had visited Benicia in July of the same year, he wrote: ". . . the City of Benicia is merely a little dull, miserable town of not over five hundred inhabitants, and were it not for the United States Arsenal and the ships of the Panama steamers, where they make their repairs, there would be nothing here." After having studied the surrounding country once owned by grantees and hearing of the seemingly unending squatter problems, he wrote: "The story of these Spanish grants is a long one, and a black one. Our central government has much to answer for . . . Political corruption has other sins to answer for as well as the rebellion at home. The great drawback on the settlement of this state has been, is now, and will be for years to come, the insecurity of land titles, and for this, southern politicians more than northern are the cause . . ." [W.H. Brewer, *op. cit,* p. 292-293].

July 18.

"I was up this morning at a very early hour and took the family to the Convent. I remained there walking in those classic groves through which many a delicate foot has trampled on, till the hour of the opening of the exhibition, 9 A.M. The examination through which the pupils passed deserves more praise than can be pronounced from the pen of a young beginner; but to return to the exhibition. It was not only my opinion, but that of a vast number, that it was a failure, but the addresses and compositions were excellent, especially one or two, which I will designate; 'The Power of Conscience' composed by Bessi Roche, and delivered by S. Edilin. It is out of place for me to put here which of the young ladies appeared to me more engaging, but I cannot restrain from taking a short note. This beauty was the 'L-im-of-m-h' (lovely image of my heart), many young ladies from the Convent, among them was Miss Kate. Came from the boat to Magdalena's. I slept at the Russ House this evening, for the first time and was bitten by the mosquitos and to my luck, Kate also stopped at the Russ House, but did not see her, it was already too late when I went to bed."

Sunday, July 20.

"I attended church services in Oakland with Lola and later enjoyed dinner with Jose Antonio Maria [J.M.'s brother] and my family. Father Guinn of St. Mary's Church and Louis Cronley were here this afternoon, from Amador they came. In the parlor this evening, Mr. Ward said he knew Dr. O'Brien very well and when I heard this I was very anxious to make Mr. O'Brien's acquaintance, Miss Kate O'Brien's father. . . ."

"Amador" was a small settlement in Alameda County; approximately eight miles east of Hayward and six miles north of Pleasanton. The community later named "Dublin" was originally a portion of Rancho Ramon granted to Jose Maria Amador in the mid 1830s. W.H. Brewer visited Amador in 1861. He wrote: "Game is very abundant—bear in the hills, and deer, antelope and elk like cattle in herds. At Amador we stopped, fed our mules and got dinner. There were two taverns, a grocery and about two houses. A horse-race was coming off in the afternoon, and a mixed crowd of fifty or a hundred American, Mexican, and Indian assembled—decidedly a hard looking crowd—drinking, swearing, betting, and gambling."

Brewer's stay in Amador was brief which accounts for having seen only about two houses. By the late 1850s Amador already boasted several attractive homes, but because they were surrounded by gardens and many trees, they were not visible from the center of the settlement. One was the home of the Estudillos' friend, Mr. James Witt Dougherty, who had purchased about ten thousand acres from Don Jose Maria Amador in about 1852. By the early 1870s, so many Irish families had arrived that the old settlement of Amador became known as *Dublin*. The Doughertys' first home stood near Alameda Springs and was built of immense redwood timbers from San Antonio Creek and was surrounded by magnificant gardens. Mr. J.W. Dougherty was born in Tennessee on April 26, 1819 and died on September 30, 1879. Eight years later, his wife, Elizabeth Argyle, was also lain to rest in Dublin's historic cemetery, which is being restored.

July 23.

"News came today on the taking of Charleston."

This was erroneous. The city of Charleston did not formally surrender until February 1865. Our diarist and others in California may have misunderstood or were ill-informed of the Union victory on July 1, 1862. This took place when Lee's last effort to disrupt McClellan's retreat was repulsed at Malvern Hill after seven days of battle, felling some 5,500 Confederates. About midnight of February 17, 1865, as the last Confederate troops were leaving Charleston, So. Carolina, they fired the upper part of the city to prevent great quantities of cotton, rice, and 200 kegs of gunpowder from falling into the hands of the Union Army. A terrific explosion took place at three o'clock on the morning of the 18th. A few hours later, the mayor of Charleston announced that the Confederate forces had withdrawn from the city and by nine 'clock of the same day, the city of Charleston formally surrendered. [John Laird Wilson *Pictorial History of the Great Civil War,* pp. 886, 887].

July 24.

"I saw Jacob Leese, we came together to see Magdalena. I invited him to see the 'Lancaster' tomorrow. . . . Before going to bed I visited the 'Fair at the Occidental' for the benefit of the Catholic Schools of San Francisco. I went to bed at twelve."

The battleship, S.S. Lancaster, then temporarily anchored in San Franciso Bay, was destroyed on March 26, 1863, attempting to pass the batteries at Vicksburg.

Jacob Leese, then twenty-three years, was the eldest son of Mr. and Mrs. Jacob Primer Leese of San Francisco. He attended Santa Clara College and later married a niece of Governor Alvarado. His father, a native of Ohio, arrived at Monterey in June, 1833, and on April 1, 1837, married Rosalia, a sister of General Mariano G. Vallejo who was opposed to the marriage. [H.H. Bancroft, *History of California*, Vol. IV, p. 710]. Mrs. Leese was one of the most charming and cultured women of her time, but despite her husband's prominence and wealth, their marriage was not a happy one.

In 1873, Mrs. Jacob Primer Leese was interviewed by Henry Cerruti, at the request of H.H. Bancroft. She related that her husband had squandered her dowry and in later years, deserted her; leaving her to care for her two sons and four daughters. Her bitter attitude towards Americans was due in part to this sorrow. [*Rambling in California—The Adventures of Henry Cerruti,* edited by Margaret Mollins and Virginia E. Thickens, p. 116.] Although her children were educated in American schools, Mrs. Leese insisted that they speak only Spanish in her presence. Her daughter, Rosalia, born on April 15, 1838, was the first white child born in what is now the great metropolis of San Franciso. [Frank Avila, *The Annals of San Francisco,* p. 201.]

July 24.

". . . I saw Leese and we came together to the wharf where I had a boat engaged to visit the warship 'Lancaster'—we remained on board about quarter of an hour or more. I was perfectly delighted with everything on board; everything looked so neat and clean. I went to visit Maria, remained a short time. This evening I went to the Opera, 'Norma' was played. In my estimation the operatic troupe did not do much credit to the celebrated opera—there I saw Miss *Kate* and she looked as charming as ever. Also I saw Mr. Sullivan with whom I spoke. I was introduced to Mrs. Sullivan. Grace Riddle had a private box!"

Sunday, July 27.

"Went to church with Mr. Ward in the small buggy, went into the garden and made a small bouquet which I took to Magdalena. I went to the house, had lunch and then came to see the clerk of the 'Brother Jonathan' about the state room for the family. After finishing my business I went home, took a bath and got ready to go to the Calico Party, which I did after supper. James was there also. I can freely say that I never saw a party of so many mad looking faces, of course with some exceptions, such as the Misses Regan. These ladies were comparatively the only ones I danced with. Taking the thing as a whole, and for those whose aid the proceeds were to go, the ball was very good, everything was over at 5 (A.M.), then James Hughes and myself went to bed at the Russ House."

The "Brother Jonathan" was one of the coastal steamers operated by the Oregon and San Francisco Steamship Line with offices at the northeast corner of Front and Jackson streets. Steamers bound for Santa Barbara, San Pedro, and San Diego left the Pacific Wharf at nine o'clock in the morning of the third and eighth day of each month. Arrangements for passage were made through Captain J. Hensley, agent for the San Francisco office. The Brother Jonathan with one hundred and ninety passengers and a fortune in gold and greenbacks was wrecked on July 31, 1865. The vessel had left San Francisco enroute to Portland, Oregon, when it struck a hidden rock during a heavy storm off the coast fo Crescent City.

The "Calico Party" was a benefit for the Roman Catholic Orphanage Asylum, known as the Mount St. Joseph's School for Girls; organized in 1852. Because tickets were reasonable and available to various classes of people, it is presumed that the "many mad looking faces" were those J.M. deemed beneath his social status or compared them with the beautiful young ladies he had seen at the opera just three days previously.

On July 29, ". . . My mother gave me to understand this evening that it would be better for Jose Ramon to go with them to Los Angeles than me because I was coming back soon, nothing was decided. . . ." Juana's change of plans may have been because it was already late July and the fall semester at Santa Clara College was to open on August 24. Under normal traveling conditions, twenty-six days was adequate, however, travel by steamer was time consuming especially if storms and heavy fogs along the coast caused delays and changes in schedule.

On the following day, J.M.'s friend, Mr. Stoakes, gave him an exceptionally fine bowie-knife; a formidable weapon often worn by travelers for defense where law and order had not been established. However, Mr. Stoakes may not have intended the gift to be used for that purpose.

Although he knew J.M. was soon to leave for southern California, W.H. Brewer and his associates were in Los Angeles in December 1860. Brewer wrote: "This southern California is still unsettled. We all continually wear arms—each wears both bowie-knife and pistol—navy revolver, while we have always for game or otherwise a Sharp's carbine, and two double-barrel shotguns. Fifty to sixty murders per year have been common here in Los Angeles, and some think it odd that there has been no violent death during the two weeks we have been here. [W.H. Brewer, *op cit,* p. 14.] Most of the murders were the result of excessive drinking among the lower class Mexicans and Indian vaqueros from the outlying ranchos who rode into the settlement on Saturdays and Sundays."

"With what feeling of emotion and desire did we at College wish for the time to come when we should once more find ourselves in the bosom of our families, now the month of July has passed, and soon our vacation will be over, and [we will] meet in the classic halls of Santa Clara College. This afternoon I shaved, this is my second time, but as yet I have not shaved my mustache."

10

Travel

Friday, August 1.

"A new month has entered, and has commenced with a very warm day. This morning some of the Millers from San Rafael passed through here to picnic at Palomares. Miss Mary Miller stopped to see Lola and returning this evening, the whole party stopped for a short time at the hotel [Estudillo House] and came into the parlor. I commenced to finish everything that was to be fixed and arranged for tomorrow."

Palomares Canyon is the beautiful course of a boulder-strewn tributary of San Lorenzo Creek which empties into Alameda Creek about three or four miles east of Niles in Alameda County. Reputedly, the canyon was named in honor of Jose Francisco Palomares, an early Indian fighter who had resided in the vicinity of Mission San Jose since 1832. The Estudillos and other picnickers often saw deer, antelope, fox and coyote on the gentle slopes, but only experienced and armed hunters dared penetrate the habitat of cougars and immense bears in the steep and thickly-wooded formations to each side of the stream a mile or two before it empties into Alameda Creek.

August 2.

"Came to the city, passed on the ten o'clock boat, my mother, Eulalia and Lola, as also Juan Vicente and Luis. My route is destined for Los Angeles. From the wharf of the Oakland boat [in San Francisco] I went to the Brother Jonathan and left their baggage. Came to the hotel and retired to rest at half past one A.M. Jose Antonio came from Washoe last night. I was introduced to Captain Seeley of the vessel, Brother Jonathan."

J.M.'s brother, Jose Antonio, was one of the thousands who were attracted to the Washoe silver mines in the Territory of Nevada. In 1860, when the mines were at their height, the excitement was known as the "Washoe Fever" and though fortunes were made by some, countless others left the area after they had lost whatever little money they had upon arrival. After another brother returned from the mines in 1864, J.M. wrote: "Jose Ramon, the poor fellow is almost ruined, both in constitution and purse."

Sunday, August 3.

"I was up very early this morning, went to Magdalena's, had breakfast and came away to the boat with all the family. I was introduced to many ladies and gentlemen, at quarter past nine we left San Francisco on the way to Los Angeles, as we came out of port, a heavy fog set in and did not see land till we came to Point Conception, but still the fog continued and the sea was very rough and the effect produced on my mother and Lola can easily be imagined, sea-sickness of course was the result, but for myself, I did not get sick at all. Eulalia also did not get sick."

In a notation in the back of his journal, J.M. had noted that his brother, Juan Vicente, had given him $100.00 towards his summer vacation just before the vessel left the wharf. Juan had given him $20.00 on the previous day, but for some unknown reason, J.M. was obliged to give his mother all but $5.00 of the amount.

August 4.

"I was up this morning very early, the exact time I do not recollect, still the fog continued, but about half past nine or ten A.M. we commenced to see the sea shore and when in the Santa Barbara Coast, the fog disappeared, and at half past twelve we arrived at Santa Barbara and anchored there till half past six or seven. I went ashore, I saw Carlos Thompson and Frank and also went to the Mission, visited the pond of water and the aqueduct, brought some orange blossoms to the boat. At half past six or seven we left. I had some good time with Miss Mary Hall, a passenger, but she acted the coquet this evening. As we left, the fog set in again and soon everything was as yesterday. I went to bed at ten o'clock."

Frank Thompson was twenty-six years of age and his brother, Carlos, was seventeen. They were the sons of Captain Alpheus Basil Thompson and his wife, the former Senorita Francisca Carrillo of Santa Barbara. Mr. Thompson, a native of Massachusetts, settled in Santa Barbara in about 1831. Most of his wealth was acquired in the 1800s when he was one of the major sea otter traders on the Pacific Coast. He also was engaged in various other remunerative activities. The Thompsons' attractive two-story adobe home of Monterey architecture, was constructed in 1834 on the west side of present State Street above de La Guerra Avenue in Santa Barbara. The Thompsons were among the settlement's wealthiest and most prominent early families. It was in front of their home that Commodore Stockton raised the Stars and Stripes in July, 1846, although California had not as yet been ceded to the United States.

While J.M. walked about Mission Santa Barbara, hundreds of swifts* darted to and from their mud nests edging the tiled roof of the crumbling structure. Dry grasses filled the nearby Moorish fountain which had served as an Indian community laundry since its construction by the Franciscan Friars in 1808. The Mission, however, is the fourth structure on the site, the third having been destroyed by the earthquake of 1812. W.H. Brewer visited Santa Barbara in 1861, and wrote that its 1,400 inhabitants were mainly the descendants of the early Mexican and Spanish families and that the town had altered little since the Mexican Period except for the waterfront which was crowded by a conglomoration of vessels, warehouses and places of business. Brewer's description enables one to visualize J.M. wandering about the extensive ruins. He wrote: "Up the canyon two or three miles a strong cement dam has been built, whence water was brought down to the Mission in an aqueduct made of stone and cement, still in good repair. Near the Mission it flows into two large tanks or cisterns, reservoirs I ought to call them, built of masonry and cement, substantial and fine. These fed a mill where grain was ground, and ran into pipes to supply the fountain in front of the church and in the gardens, and thence to irrigate the cultivated slope beneath. But now all is in ruin—the fountain dry, the pipes broken, weeds growing in the cisterns and basins. I find it hard to realize that I am an American in the United States, the young and vigorous republic as we call it here when I see these ruins. They carry me back again to the Old World with its decline and decay. . . ." [W.H. Brewer, *op cit,* pp. 57-58.]

August 5.

"I was awakened this morning about half past two or three o'clock by

---

* Undoubtedly barn swallows (*Hirundo rustica*—Ed.)

the noise of the steamer, which had just anchored at San Pedro and by four, all were up, took breakfast and then came away to land in a small steamer. I was very busy all the time with the baggage. Miss Hall sat close to us in the steamer from the Brother Jonathan to the land, and at the land we took the same stage to Los Angeles and had a very pleasant time. We were opposite each other in the stage, indeed the road seemed to me a very short one. We left the landing at quarter to six and got to Los Angeles at ten minutes to nine, or there abouts. We stopped at Mr. Dalton's house. I was in the orchard this afternoon, ate plenty of fruit. I was at the Bella Union Hotel and Miss Hall had already gone to San Gabriel."

Mr. Phineas T. Banning's small steamers conveyed passengers and their baggage from the coastal vessels anchored in the deep waters of the Pacific, to his wharf at the mouth of a stream, which according to R.H. Dana, Jr. was ". . . in a quiet place, safe from southeasters." [R.H. Dana, Jr., *op cit,* p. 446, 1887 edition.] The small steamers were, however, often confronted with problems that equalled those of the coastal vessels. In 1863, one was caught in a sudden gale and its boiler exploded; Mr. Banning was miraculously blown onto a submerged sandbar. He was later rescued, but the other fifty-three passengers were either injured, killed by the blast, or drowned. Among the lost passengers were J.M.'s friend, Miss Minerva Hereford of Los Angeles, and Captain Seeley of the Brother Jonathan. [Maymie Krythe, *Past Admiral-Phineas Banning,* 1830-1888, p. 115-116.]

After Dana travelled the same route in 1857, he wrote: "I got a seat on the top of the coach, to which were tackled six less than wild California horses. Each horse had a man at his head, and when the driver got his reins in hand and gave the word, all horses were let go at once, and away they went on a spring, tearing over the ground, the driver only keeping them from going the wrong way, for they had a wide, level pampas to run over the whole thirty miles to the Pueblo . . ." [Dana, *op cit,* p. 447, 1887 edition.] "As we changed horses twice, we did not slacken our speed until we turned into the streets of the Pueblo."

After almost three hours of travel, without stopping to water the sweating horses, the stage finally stopped at the Bella Union Hotel on Main Street in Los Angeles. Miss Alma was met by her father, Mr. Franklin Hall, in a handsome surrey to convey his comely daughter to their beautiful home in the vicinity of Mission San Gabriel. The Estudillos were greeted by Mr. and Mrs. Henry Dalton and taken to their attractive home in Los Angeles although they usually spent the summer months at their Azusa Rancho. Mrs. Dalton was Eulalia Estudillo's sister, the former Guadalupe Zamorano. Mr. Dalton, commonly known as Enrique, was a 64 year old man, English by birth and had lived in Los Angeles for many years. He became a Mexican citizen shortly after 1844 when he arrived in California. In 1862, his vineyard in the San Gabriel District was valued at some twenty thousand dollars, however he had already been forced to sell some of his vast holdings to meet costly litigations upon the infiltration of squatters.

By 1862, law and order had wiped out most of the ugly scenes earlier travelers were apt to witness in the settlement. For years, its sordid reputation equaled or exceeded that of any gold-rush communities. In 1854, only eight years before the Estudillos arrived, a visitor wrote: "It was not an infrequent thing to find a dead Indian on the street in the morning, in some parts of the city." [Reverette James Woods, *Recollections of Pioneer Work in California,* p. 203.] During the remaining year, Los Angeles was a fairly respectable community, but by 1860, an encampment of troops was deemed necessary because many of its inhabitants were avid secessionists.

Despite the numerous vineyards, orchards, and orange groves in the outlying country, few of the lower-class citizens of Los Angeles were able to afford to purchase the fruit. Brewer wrote: ". . . fruit plenty in the streets, but very dear—apples four to fifteen cents each, oranges five to ten cents." [Brewer, *op cit,* p. 40.] Merchants demanded the same price for home-grown fruits and vegetables as those hauled from Northern counties. Barley and some fruits from San Diego County were costlier than those shipped from San Francisco.

August 6.

"Wrote two letters, one to Juan and another to Vicente, the one to Juan was a very long one, I gave him a very long account of the trip. This afternoon, Charles Webber let me have a horse and a saddle and I started at four o'clock for Rowland's Ranch, La Puente."

Charles W. Webber, a native of New York who had arrived in California very young, married Mary H. Hawkins in 1863. She was the widow of R.T. Hawkins who had lost his life when a conflagration enveloped the vessel *Golden Gate* in July 1862, while on his way east to enlist in the United States Army. Shortly after their marriage, Mr. and Mrs. C.W. Webber moved to San Leandro where they purchased the Beatty Hotel and renamed it the *Webber House*. The large two-story hotel was located on the Northwest side of present Clarke Street between Davis and present West Estudillo Avenue. Mr. Webber died in 1864, while visiting his relatives in Los Angeles. After his death, his widow continued to operate the *Webber House.*

"When on my way, I asked the route of many persons and by half past six I arrived at Mr. Rowland's house. Tonight Bob Cunningham came home very late. I made Miss Gray's acquaintance and enjoyed the evening very well. I smoked many cigarritos given me by Mary [Gray]. I went to bed this evening rather late."

August 7.

"I was up this morning rather late, took breakfast and went around the vineyard for some time, shooting with my pistol. At one P.M., William Rowland, Bob Cunningham and myself and most of the vaqueros went to the San Gabriel River to bring some steers which we brought to the corral, but we had a great trouble putting them into the corral."

Early ranchers often grazed their cattle for extended periods in the remote areas of their holdings. They had learned through experience that cattle in their acquired wild state, were less subject to attacks by cougars or cattle rustlers. However, round-ups were hazardous when half-wild herds often became more dangerous than bears or cougars. No vaquero dared be among them unmounted. Riders were slow in their movements and remained as quiet as possible for fear of exciting the unpredictable animals. If a vaquero sensed excitement, he frequently began to sing or hum in low, monotonous tones which had a quieting effect upon the herd. W.H. Brewer rode through ranchos in southern California in the early 1860s and wrote: "On these ranches, as there are no fences, the cattle are half-wild, and require many horses to keep them and tend them. A ranch with a thousand head of cattle will have a hundred horses." [W.H. Brewer, *op cit*, p. 44.]

"I found a note in my room left by Miss Mary telling me that I had broken a promise, not being at home in the afternoon at four for dinner. This evening I enjoyed the time very well. Miss Mary told me some things about Miss Woodworth [of San Francisco], that she had a card with my name when she was at Miss Atkin's Academy in Benicia. This card I never gave it, she probably got it from Mrs. Nugent."

Mary Gray was born in Kentucky in 1843. Jealousy was aroused when Miss Woodworth proudly showed her one of J.M.'s "Carte De

Visites" which probably led Mary to believe that Miss Woodworth was, or had been, the recipient of his attentions. Miss Woodworth was a member of a prominent San Francisco family and educated at Benicia's Young Ladies Seminary, conducted by Miss Mary Atkins in 1862.

August 9.

"Soon after breakfast, the riding horses of Miss Gray and myself were gotten ready and we left the Ranch on our way to Mr. Hall's at San Gabriel. On our way to the Mission, I inquired of her who had been the teacher at 'El Monte,' but she would not tell me until this evening while sitting in the parlor. At Mr. Hall's I saw Miss Hall and of course her giddiness was soon manifested. The opinion formed by Miss Mary of the young lady was not a very high one. In this I followed suit. We had dinner with Mr. Hall and came home at six, the evening was very beautiful, a very clear moonlight. James Gray and Bob Cunningham were with us when going home. James was, I am very sorry to say, very tipsy. This evening was one that I have never enjoyed better in my life with a very pleasant companion, and remained up till one o'clock. I passed a happy time, being my last night to remain on the Ranch."

El Monte was a small, private school located in a settlement bearing the same name between San Gabriel and Los Angeles. It also had a sordid reputation and was a hot bed of secessionists during the Civil War. W.H. Brewer rode through this country in 1861 and wrote: "We passed over the lovely plains of San Gariel, El Monte and Los Angeles, with their thousands of cattle, horses, and sheep feeding; tens of thousands were to be seen. . . ." [W.H. Brewer, *op cit,* p. 40.]

J.M. and Mary Gray's moonlight ride back to Rancho La Puente was undoubtedly enchanting. However, most all of early California's romances were blessed by beautiful settings, perfumed by lemon-verbena, roses and honeysuckle vines. When J.M.'s cousin Elena of San Diego was being courted by Joseph W. Wolfskill of Los Angeles, he was obliged to ride the entire distance on a mule. His token of love was as simple as his mode of travel. Once, he chanced upon a bed of wild roses hugging a spring a short distance from San Diego. Here he tethered his mule, cut several of the most beautiful blooms, and placed them carefully upon his baggage and rode onward. By the time he arrived at Casa de Pedrorena the leaves and delicate roses had withered beyond recognition. The next time Joseph left Los Angeles, he placed a large raw potato among his belongings and when he again reached the spring, cut and placed each sprig of rose deeply into the watery tuber and rode onward. At Elena's home, his eyes beamed with pride as he presented her with the delightfully-fresh bouquet, quite in contrast to the weary suitor and the sweating animal.

On August 10, he again visited Miss Hall and "I made out that she had kissed Mr. Howard the other night on a walk although she denied to me ever having kissed anybody. From there I came to town [Los Angeles]. This evening we had some different kinds of games in the parlor."

Notations in J.M.'s later journals reveal his close observations of young ladies and his critical character. ". . . at the piano she puts on too many airs." Another read: ". . . she is very pleasant, rather good looking and converses well." After another social function where he met a beautiful American girl, he wrote: ". . . a very accomplished young lady, and perfectly lady-like in her actions, including in this respect very much to the Spanish character." From the latter quotation, one may conclude that he was especially fond of Mary Gray because her refinement and social grace reminded him of his well-bred sisters, and his acquaintances at San Jose's Convent of Notre Dame, especially Miss Grace Riddle of San Francisco.

11

Journey to San Diego

On the morning of August 12, 1862, J.M. deposited ten dollars at the Department of the San Diego-Los Angeles Stage Company for his long anticipated journey to San Diego. With the ticket clutched tightly in his hand, he was soon to realize he had placed himself at the mercy of a bouncing vehicle, a cursing whip-lashing driver and a scorching August sun. He did not know however that he had not more than an even chance of having his journey delayed or even discontinued while enroute. As his baggage was being thrown on top of the stage, his mother called out last minute advice to her excited son. His journey commenced with a resounding crack of the whip and waving farewell to the Daltons, Lola, Eulalai and his mother as the first clouds of dust rose from the spinning wheels.

Upon the establishment of California's stage lines in the early 1850s, one of the major problems was the leasing or purchasing of the land edging the proposed route where at intervals, barns were to be constructed to serve as change-stations. These were to accommodate fresh horses, wheels, axles and other stage equipment. If a suitable structure was found near the roadway, it was leased from the owner and whenever possible, arrangements were made whereby he would board travelers if the roadway could easily be seen and approached from the landowner's dwelling.

Change-stations in California were usually placed about twenty to thirty-five miles apart depending upon the contour and surface of the country. If four or less travelers occupied the stage, four horses were deemed adequate, but if great sandy areas or steep grades lay ahead, six were hitched to the vehicle. Occasionally, even this number proved to be unsatisfactory. It was not uncommon for drivers of the Los Angeles and San Diego lines to unhitch their worn horses and search the countryside for oxen to extricate the vehicle from bottomless mud or sand according to season. Male passengers were expected to assist the driver, who invariably dispensed with his usual meager courtesies and proper language. B.I. Hayes, a frequent traveler between Los Angeles and San Diego, wrote: "Why stage drivers, who are paid a liberal stipend per month for putting passengers over public highways, should be so vindictively hostile to the traveling community surpasses my comprehension." [B.I Hayes, *op. cit.* (loose papers).]

After ten and one half hours of traveling, J.M.'s stage stopped for the night at San Juan Capistrano. Although he was exceedingly tired, he mustered up enough energy to write in his journal before retiring. "Left Los Angeles this morning at eight o'clock in the stage on my way to San Diego, a lady accompanied us. I was the only other passenger besides her. After four or five hours of travel, we arrived at Anaheim where we dined; this was our first station where we changed horses, two wild mares were put to the stage; these did not last long without getting tired and we had great trouble making them go. After many hardships, we arrived at San Juan Capistrano at half past six P.M. I stopped at the house of Mr. Foaster [Forster] where I heard a great narration of the doings of a man who names himself Andronico Vallejo. A short time after tea, I retired to rest. I hadn't been in bed but one or two hours, when Alejandro Forbes and Carlos came into the room.

"We met the Dogles about two miles this side of the San Gabriel River." Because J.M frequently misspelled names, the "Dogles" were probably Mr. and Mrs. Doyle of San Diego, who were on their way to Los Angeles. In 1859, when R.H. Dana, Jr. was in San Diego, he wrote: "I found an American family here with whom I dined, Doyle and his wife, nice young couple, Doyle agent for the great line of coaches to run to the frontier from the old States." [R.H. Dana, Jr., *op. cit.*, p. 451, 1887 edition.] This line of coaches was the *Missouri California Overland Stage Line* established in 1858, to run via the southern plains route between St. Louis and San Francisco on a twenty-five day schedule.

"I was told that my letter to Guadalupe had been left with Mr. Pedleton [Pendleton] for Guadalupe and was not at San Diego. I shot a rabbit with my pistol. One of the wheels of the stage passed over my foot and tonight it pained me a great deal."

This injury probably occurred while J.M was assisting the stage driver with the "two wild mares" that were hitched to the vehicle at the Anaheim change station. This small settlement was located about thirty miles south of Los Angeles and comprised mainly of German colonists, who in 1857, established the noted grape industry of southern California. Despite the comparative flat country between Los Angeles and Anaheim, the horses were whipped unmercifully to prevent the vehicle from sinking into the loose surface. Beatings were often useless. In the same year, 1862, one of Phineas Banning's six-horse stages could not be extricated from the sandy surface until oxen had been hitched to the vehicle. But the most hazardous areas were where numerous deep ruts crossed the route, the result of the January downpours, when it rained incessantly for twenty eight days in southern California. The seriousness of road conditions appeared in a letter B.I. Hayes received from a friend in January of that year. It reads in part: "It has been raining three weeks in San Bernardino. My road is all washed away; all my former work is lost. I now have to make a new road or lose all that I have expended. Some people advise me to quit road-building, but I am determined to build a road at all hazards."

The stage route from Los Angeles southward was about twelve miles west of the *Camino Real,* but joined the ancient roadway near the present town of El Toro about ten miles northeast of San Juan Capistrano. From there it continued southward and for the most part a little east of present State Highway 101. [B.I. Hayes, *op. cit.,* (loose papers).]

J.M.'s host at San Juan Capistrano was Mr. John Forster, then about forty-eight years, and known to the Californios as "Don Juan." He arrived in California from his native England in 1833, and four years later, married Ysadora Pico, a sister of Andres and Pio Pico. In 1862, the Forsters were living temporarily in one of the few remaining structures of Mission San Juan Capistrano. The Camino Real fronted the ruins of Mission's first Chapel, but the stage route lay a little west of the ancient courtyard of the Forsters' quarters.

Mission San Juan Capistrano, the 7th of California's religious establishments, was formally established in November, 1776 and is presently located on Interstate Highway 5. The town of San Juan Capistrano evolved after the secularization of the Mission in October, 1834. Because the Mexican government had resolved to convert California's missions into pueblos, San Juan Capistrano became known as *Pueblo de San Juan de Arguello* in 1838, when Don Santiago Arguello, Sr., was appointed administrator of the Mission.

In December 1845, John Forster and James McKinley purchased the abandoned mission structures and gardens from Governor Pico Pico upon a public notice for the sale to the highest bidder. This, however, did not include the shell of the first chapel damaged during the terrifying earthquake shocks of 1812, or the second chapel, with its graceful arches and lengthy corridors, which was claimed by the Catholic Church. In 1844, Governor Manual Micheltorena authorized the sale of mission properties to raise funds for defense against a possible war between Mexico and the United States, declared in May 1846.

Some years later, the United States Government refused confirmation of Forster's claim to the mission structures, but upheld his claim to the adjacent ranchos. Present San Juan Capistrano takes pride in its colorful past, its picturesque mission, the Garcia House, and the small, adobe home on Calle de Los Rios. This humble, but tidy dwelling has been occupied by the Rios family for over a century and bears a California State Historical Marker.

Apparently, J.M. was quite annoyed by the "great narration" of the doings of Andronico Jose Vallejo who was ten years older than J.M., and the eldest son of Mariano Guadalupe Vallejo, the most influential man in California during the Mexican Period. Andronico was well educated, an accomplished violinist and undoubtedly, an interesting guest although not appreciated by the self-centered eighteen year old traveler. Well-read Vallejo chose illustrious names for his sons. Andronico was taken from Shakespeare's drama *Titus Andronicus*.

San Juan Capistrano. August 13.

"I was called up this morning by the stage driver at five o'clock A.M., got ready and went to where the stage was, took a cup of coffee and soon after, we left San Juan where A. Forbes got in the stage with us [J.M. and the woman passenger] and we went to San Diego." San Juan Capistrano's first stage station was a small shed west of the mission structures. The stage line later constructed several sheds, an immense water trough and a large barn to the rear of an adobe dwelling built in the early 1840s by Manuel Garcia. One finds in Helen S. Griffin's *Casas and Courtyards* that some years after Garcia left San Juan Capistrano, his home was acquired by a Domingo Oyharzabal, who converted it into the French Hotel and added a balcony to the upper story. This is where the woman traveler and the stage driver remained for the night while J.M. and Alejandro enjoyed the Forsters' hospitality. At present, the former hotel is a private home about two blocks south of the mission and known as the Garcia House.

J.M. added: "From San Juan we took a south western direction and came to the sea shore and traveled by the sea about three or four miles. We walked about a mile through the sand. We passed the San Mateo Rancho. On our way through the sea shore, I shot many times at some species of fish, also rabbits. We passed through many beautiful ranchos such as Las Flores and the splendid Rancho Santa Margarita, where we bought a watermelon."

At present, Camp Pendleton, the world's largest Marine Base, occupies 132 thousand acres of former Rancho Santa Margarita y Las Flores. In spring, the soft slopes and portions of the lowlands are carpeted with lush grasses, golden poppies, scarlet paintbrush, purplish-red owl's clover and other wild flowers. J. Ross Brown traveled through this area in 1851. On page 231 in his *Crusoe's Island* we read: "There is nothing comparable to the mingled wilderness and repose of such a scene." Never, during his travels in Europe had he ever encountered more beautiful country.

"At the hill of St. Marg., we had to use a pair of oxen to pull us up the hill because the horses were tired. We got to San Luis Rey about quarter passed one P.M. Took dinner at Mr. Thibitt's [Tibbetts'] house where we took fresh horses and left about two o'clock. Our next stop was at the Encinitas Ranch. From there we traveled at a furious rate and the consequence was that the horses did not last long without getting tired. Never in my life had I seen so many hares, rabbits, quails and other small hunting game as I saw on the road."

During the summer months, stage-drivers frequently abandoned their usual route if the ocean was at ebb tide to follow the hard, damp surface of the shoreline. This was to cool the sweating horses, uncomfortable travelers and to escape from the choking clouds of dust of the inland route. The detour often presented difficulties which necessitated travelers to walk behind the stage until the axles were again well above the surface. Travelers in light, private conveyances rarely sank into the sand. When Mr. Hayes and his companion rode the shoreline on horseback in 1857, they were amazed when a light vehicle was seen skipping along the waters' edge at eight miles per hour.

East of present Carlsbad, thirty-five miles north of San Diego, and a short distance south of the Mission, was a small change station owned and operated by Mr. & Mrs. George Tibbetts, the only American family residing in this exceptionally beautiful valley. Mrs. Tibbetts, a daughter of Juan Rodriquez of San Diego, maintained the humble Inn with amazing·ability. Mr. B.I. Hayes stopped there in 1857, and noted her well-clothed and mannerly children and while Mr. Tibbetts was working in the fields, she assisted stage-drivers by leading the jaded horses to pasture. If Mr. Hayes was favorably impressed, one may imagine how much this stopping place must have pleased the dust-laden woman traveler, especially when she found an immense, ironstone bowl and pitcher of cold, clear water and bar of homemade soap and a spotless towel neatly folded on the towel rack. What a sigh of relief she must have given upon realizing that for awhile at least, J.M. and Alejandro Forbes had to put aside the pistols which for miles had made her cringe with each report.

Four or five miles south of Rancho Las Encinitas, the stage route cut through Rancho San Dieguito, keeping some distance inland and west of a broad, sandy valley. Rancho San Dieguito derived its Spanish name from "little creek of Saint Diego," and not from the Diegueno Indians, the only tribe that inhabited present San Diego County. Because these natives had no name of their own, the early Spanish explorers named them *Dieguenos*. [A.L. Krober, *Handbook of California Indians,* p. 709.] At present a portion of this historic rancho is known as *Rancho Santa Fe* which dates from 1906, when the Santa Fe Land Company purchased the property. It developed into one of California's most beautiful and exclusive residential areas.

Although the general course was southward, the driver circled around a large marshy area before fording the sluggish waters of the San Dieguito [or San Bernardino River] and Peñasquito Creek that cut through Rancho Los Peñasquito. Rancho Los Peñasquitos (the little cliffs) was the first grant in present San Diego County and acquired by Captain Francisco Maria Ruiz in June 1823.

For almost twenty-five miles before reaching the San Diego River, the Camino Real kept close to the coast, however, the country was largely barren with only a scattering of shrubbery and thirsty pines of inconsequential size that had not received a drop of moisture since the sudden termination of spring downpours. Fortunately for the aching travelers, the termination of the journey wasn't far off. About three or four miles northeast of Old Town San Diego, the stage forded the San Diego River.

At the San Diego stage-station, J.M. and Alejandro were met by J.M.'s cousin, Jose Antonio Estudillo, who only accompanied them to the home of Mrs. Estefana Johnson. Because the notation in his journal that evening did not please him, he later wrote of his arrival on a separate piece of paper and inserted it in back of his diary. It reads: "Arrived at the town of San Diego at half past eight o'clock. Stopped at the hotel and from there I was taken to the house of Mrs. Johnson where I remained for the night. There I met Mrs. C. Pedleton [Pendleton], Mrs. Johnson, Dona Rosario Aguirre, Maria Antonia Arguello and another lady whose acquaintance I did not make. The long drive and hardship of the road took a great effect on me, that of being very tired for the evening."

Because J.M. failed to give the full name of his hostess the evening of his arrival, she probably was Mrs. George Alonzo Johnson or *Estefana* as she was known among her relatives and intimate friends. Estefana was the daughter of Don Francisco Maria Alvarado and his wife, Tomasa Pico of San Diego. The other Mrs. Johnson at the welcoming may have been Mrs. Charles R. Johnson, the former Maria de la Dolores, daughter of Don Juan Bandini and his second wife, Refugio Arguello. J.M.'s cousin, Concepcion Estudillo, was the wife of George Allan Pendleton, a graduate of West Point, who had settled in Old Town in 1855. Concepcion died at the age of twenty in June 1863. Mr. Pendleton who later remarried died in March 1871, at the age of forty-eight. [Biographical files, San Diego Historical Society.] Also at the party was J.M.'s aunt, Dona Maria del Rosario Estudillo, who married Don Jose Antonio Aguirre sometime after the death of his first wife, Maria Francisco, a sister of Maria del Rosario. The gayest guests were probably J.M.'s cousins, Maria Antonia and Maria del Refugio, the daughters of Dona Guadalupe Jacoba Estudillo and her late husband, Don Santiago Emigdio Arguello.

The hotel was the Cosmopolitan in the center of Old Town San Diego. The name "Old Town" was not applied to this portion of present San Diego until 1850, when W.H. Davis and his associates established a community about one and one-half miles southwest of the ancient settlement and named their project "New Town." Although it was absorbed by the present metropolis, only "Old Town" has retained its identity. The Cosmopolitan was a large, adobe structure that had been the home of Don Juan Bandini, who completed it in 1829 for his wife, Maria de los Dolores Damiana Estudillo. Prior to 1829, Don Juan Bandini and his first wife, Maria de los Dolores Damiana Estudillo, lived at the San Diego Presidio, where their first child was born. According to Mission San Diego's Baptismal Record, Vol. 2, Number 5520, August 23, 1823, the infant was named *Maria Josefa Ramona Maximiana*. The translated border notation reads: "A little white girl from the San Diego Presidio." By the early 1830s, most of the families from Presidio Hill had moved down to present Old Town San Diego.

Sometime after her death, Bandini married Senorita Refujia, a daughter of Santiago Arguello, Sr. Some years later, the historic home was purchased by Mr. A Seeley, who added a second story with a balcony and converted it into a hotel.

The nearby stage-depot was also of adobe and had been a dramshop operated by Andres Ybarra; grantee of Rancho Las Encinitas. Old Town San Diego was indeed unattractive. It was, as R.H. Dana saw it in 1859, ". . . still like Santa Barbara, a Mexican town" and had changed little since his first visit in 1835. When B.I. Hayes compiled his *Notes on California Affairs,* he wrote that when Commodore Stockton entered the harbor of San Diego in 1846, he was entertained in a grand manner by the Bandinis. [R.H. Dana, Jr., *op. cit.,* p. 123, 450, 1887 edition.] At that time, the most prominent structures were the adobe homes of the Bandini, Pico, Arguello, Estudillo and Carrillo families. Here dashing Mariano Guadalupe Vallejo met and later married Senorita Maria Fransisca Benicia, the daughter of Joaquin Carrillo and his wife, Maria Ygnacia Lopez.

August 14

"Wrote a letter to my mother from San Diego. I was up this morning at eight o'clock A.M. I felt exceedingly tired after the traveling of the previous day. Took breakfast and then walked to different places in town. I went to see Mrs. Concepcion Pedleton [Pendleton]. I was at the house for four hours, took dinner with them and soon after, Antonio Estudillo arrived in an express wagon and I rode with him to the Point, as did Alejandro. On our way we shot sixteen shots with our pistols at different kinds of game; killed only one rabbit. We arrived at the Point about six P.M. Here I met many aunts and cousins. Lists of cousins; young ladies; Miss Maria Antonia, Gertrudis and Tulita Arguello, Dolores Estudillo and Guadalupe Arguello. Aunts—Francisca Estudillo, Magdalena Estudillo, sick in bed since 1852, and Jose Antonio Arguello."

J.M.'s walk in Old Town was indeed brief. Dusty roadways led to less than 20 well-cared homes and walled-in gardens. The outskirts of the community were largely a scattering of small, neglected orchards, ancient adobe walls, partially demolished sheds, and intermittent fencings only in shadows on the parched land. During the winter rains of late 1861 and early 1862, Union troops had been ordered to search Old Town and surroundings for firewood to provide warmth and fuel for cooking at their quarters in New Town which housed about seven hundred troops and officers. Because fencings and portions of sheds were being piled high on wagons, the inhabitants of Old Town complained about the destruction of their properties to the commanding officer. It was, he said, unfortunate, but a necessity of great military importance. [W.H. Davis, *op. cit.,* p. 554.] This was because several skirmishes had taken place in the Territory of New Mexico which Federal troops insisted upon occupying. The possibility of advancement into southern California would be welcomed by those who favored secession.

The "Point" mentioned by J.M. was La Punta, the Hacienda and cattle range of southern California's Arguello family, who at one time owned about 13,314 acres; largely of unimproved land. La Punta edged the southeastern shore of San Diego Bay and the northern end of Rancho Milijo, granted to Dona Guadalupe's late husband, Santiago Emigdio Arguello in 1834. Dona Guadalupe Jacoba Eugenia Estudillo de Arguello was born at the Monterey Presidio on November 27, 1812. [Mission Carmel Baptismal Records, Vol. 1, Entry No. 2862, November 27, 1812.]

Because Americans and Europeans were already attempting to grab acreage in present San Diego County, Governor Figueroa stipulated that Santiago Emigdio Arguello's thirty-square mile grant was not to be sold, transferred or mortgaged. [*Ibid.*] Don Santiago Emigdio Arguello was nicknamed *Santiaguito* to distinguish him from his illustrious father, Don Santiago Arguello, who had acquired vast acreage in southern California before and after the secularization of California's missions. [*Union Trust Topics,* Vol. IV, No. 6, November-December 1950, p. 2.]

The nine-room adobe dwelling, La Punta, was constructed in about 1837 and stood on a knoll about one mile east of San Diego Bay and near the mouth of the Otay River. The Otay River derived its name from the Diegueno Indian word for "brushy." [A.L. Krober's *Handbook of California Indians,* p. 896.] The name La Punta dates back to the early 1600s when Sebastian Vizcaino named the largely-barren expanse "La Punta de Buijarras." This was, however, about sixty years after Juan Rodriguez Cabrillo sailed into San Diego Bay, which was later named by Vizcaino. A Spanish map of 1782 locates "Ry Ranca de la Punta" near the southeastern bank of an unnamed stream emptying into San Diego Bay and marks the site of two Indian settlements edging the north bank of the watercourse.

According to Bancroft, the high ground just east of the south end of San Diego Bay was named *La Punta* by Don Juan Pantoja y Arriola in

1813, while mapping the shore of the bay and that it was the site of a large Indian *rancheria*. However, first white visitors to visit this area were probably Father Antonio de la Ascension and Sebastian Vizcaino, who explored the fringes of the bay in 1602. Although the colonies of Indians had been abandoned by the early 1830s, cruel, loathsome natives still lurked in the Otay Mountains east of la Punta. The early padres found that of all California's natives, the Indians of present San Diego County were the most difficult to Christianize. [Bancroft's Works, *op. cit.*, Vol. 1, p. 456.]

About three miles south of Old Town, a wagon road from the main route to Mexico led to the Arguello's adobe structures about seven miles southwest of Old Town. Because only one dwelling edged the road to La Punta, J.M. and Forbes fired their pistols with abandon. J.M. noted this vast expanse of desert-like land, but in respect of his host, remained silent. Sometime later, however, he wrote: "The soil of this country is the minest [*sic*] for cultivation that one can find. Hardly is it possible to sew barley or wheat. The vegetation is very dry. What is most sewed in that place is corn. The only fruit they have are watermelons and mush-mellons. As for pares [*sic*] and other fruit, which in our Alameda County are abundant, there they are not to be seen. Once in a while a few pares [*sic*] are brought from the San Diego Mission, but they are hardly worth the eating." Less than one hundred years later, San Diego's agricultural products reached approximately one hundred million dollars annually.

The "meanest country" was soon forgotten, but never the genuine warmth of his unassuming southern relatives.

12

La Punta and Rancho La Tia Juana

August 15.

"I was not up at a very early hour. Some time after breakfast, Jose Antonio got the express wagon ready to go to the La Tia Juana and Forbes and myself left the house with him. After an hour of traveling we came to the line that divides this State from Mexico; a brick monument stands here, but has been thrown down by some rascal Mexican, as I have heard. I got on top of this memorial at twenty minutes after ten o'clock and soon I was in Mexico. We remained at the Ranch (La Tia Juana) until four o'clock in the afternoon when we came home, on the way we hunted and I killed two rabbits, one hare and four quails. Jose killed about eighteen quails, got home about eight o'clock. Forbes remained with Jose Maria Bandini."

Jose Maria Bandini was named in honor of his grandfather, a widower of Italian descent, who left Lima, Peru in about 1820. His son, Juan, was the only one of his several children to accompany him. Before journeying to San Diego, Don Jose Maria Bandini and his son enjoyed the lavish life of Mexico City's elite society.

By 1822, Don Jose Maria Bandini had established permanent residence in San Diego, and in the same year, his son, Juan, married Maria de los Dolores Damiana Estudillo, a sister of Don Jose Joaquin Estudillo. Mission San Diego's baptismal records show that their children, Maria Josefa Ramona Maximiana, Maria Antonia Francisca de Paula, Arcadia, Ysidora, Alejandro Felix Raphael, Jose Maria, and Juan Bautista Antonio de Padua were baptized in the chapel of the San Diego Presidio. Don

109

Juan Bandini's wife died in November 1833, shortly after the birth of her last child, Juan Bautista, who was nicknamed *Juanito.*

Sometime later, Don Juan Bandini married Refugio Arguello, a daughter of Don Santiago Arguello and his wife, Maria del Pilar Ortega. Children by this marriage were Maria Dolores, Juan de la Cruz, Alfredo and Arturo. R.H. Dana, Jr. met the family in 1836 and wrote that Senora Bandini was a beautiful woman and that her husband was refined in every respect, and had the bearing of a man of birth and figure despite his financial difficulties.

Although Don Juan Bandini appeared to remain neutral during the war with Mexico, he actually favored American annexation. By the mid 1850s he had lost most of his vast holdings, money and self-respect and was no longer the social lion of southern California. He died on November 4, 1859 at the age of fifty-nine in the Los Angeles home of his daughter, Arcadia, the wife of wealthy Don Able Stearns. [Biographical files, *Bandini,* San Diego Historical Society.]

"This evening we had great fun with a bat. I made him smoke a cigarrito. Tonight I could not go to sleep for a while on account of the howling dogs."

The border monument mentioned was one of several that had been defaced or destroyed by vandals and resentful Mexicans after the close of the war with Mexico.

From 1892 through 1895, all border monuments were replaced by sturdier structures of a uniform pattern and iron gratings were placed about the base to protect them from malicious and thoughtless defacement. At present, a substantial and well-guarded border marker stands near the San Ysidro railroad station in San Diego County and about two blocks to the east as one enters Tijuana, Mexico from the United States.

Rancho La Tia Juana was granted to Santiago Arguello, Sr., in 1829 by Governor Milijo of Baja, California, probably as a reward for his military services, but less than ten years later, some 26,000 acres were abandoned owing to repeated Indian raids.

In Leonard Pitt's *The Decline of the Californios,* between 1836 and 1839, entire ranchos in present San Diego County were abandoned owing to attacks by demoralized mission Indians and their equally brutal brethren. Juan Bandini's Rancho Guadalupe near La Tia Juana was not spared.

The grant lay on both sides of the Arroyo de la Tia Juana and extended from its rugged, eastern boundary to the Pacific Ocean and northward into present San Diego County. Nellie Van De Grift Sanchez' *Spanish and Indian Names in California* gives the origin of the name *Tia Juana*. "This is an example of the corruption, through its resemblance in sound, of the Indian word "Tiwana" into Tia Juana, Spanish for 'Aunt Jane.' Tiwana is said to mean 'by the sea,' which may or may not be the correct translation." Fr. Zephyrin Engelhardt states that Tia Juana belonged to La Punta and that "an old Spanish map of Mexico has Tiguna, not Tia Juana which may be a corruption of the former or perhaps a joke, Tia Juana meaning Aunt Jane." [Fr. Zephyrin Engelhardt, *San Diego Mission,* p. 279.]

Don Santiago Arguello, Sr., was born at the Monterey Presidio on July 25, 1791, and entered the Spanish military forces at the age of eighteen. His first assignment was at the Presidio of San Francisco where his father, Jose Dario, had served as commander in 1787. Upon the death of J.M.'s paternal grandfather, Captain Jose Maria Estudillo in 1830, Lt. Santiago Arguello was placed in command of the San Diego garrison, a post he held for five years. [Bancroft's Works, *op. cit.,* Vol. 1, p. 470.] Arguello had about fourteen brothers and sisters. Most prominent in the annals of California are Don Luis Antonio Arguello, California's first Governor under Mexican rule, and Maria de la Concepcion Marcela, who in 1851, at the age of sixty, became California's first native-born daughter to receive the Dominican Habit. [Fr. Zephyrin Engelhardt, *op. cit.,* pp. 264, 404.]

Santiago Arguello, Sr., his wife, Maria Del Pilar Ortega, and their many children had lived north of the present Mexican border until 1835 upon his retirement from military and governmental duties. According to Mission San Diego Baptismal Records, Vol. II, Entry No. 5848, December 2, 1825, the name *Maria del Pilar Ortega* is also recorded in other mission records. In 1835, after Don Santiago Arguello had retired as Captain of the San Diego Presidio, he was elected *Alcalde* of San Diego. [Bancroft's Works, *op. cit.,* Vol. III, p. 608.] Sometime later, he constructed a sprawling abode dwelling and other structures on the north bank of Arroyo de La Tia Juana, then a deep, everflowing stream. Arguello's main building stood in the vicinity of present Agua Caliente.

The ailing Arguello died at the age of seventy, three months after J.M.'s visit. Arguello was eighteen when he married Maria del Pilar Ortega, a native of Santa Barbara, in 1810. Despite having given birth to twenty-two children under almost primitive conditions, Maria del Pilar outlived her husband by sixteen years, dying in 1878.

In 1862, 26,000 acres of present Tijuana were deeded to ailing Don Santiago Arguello by Mexico's President Benito Juarez. By then, squatters had already claimed much of the acreage. In 1929 when the Mexican Government declared the land patrimony of the nation, it began doling out titles to the plots occupied by the residents. Arguello's heirs then went to court and began a complicated legal fight that dragged on for more than three decades. [Time Magazine, Vol. 82, No. 13, September 27, 1963, pp. 24, 25.]

In 1962, the Mexican court finally ruled in favor of the heirs, and in the following year, a Tijuana Judge ordered the decision carried out. With this, the California Realty Company said that it would sell only 6,000 acres of unoccupied land in and around Tijuana, an estimated value of $48.5 million. [H.H. Bancroft, *Pioneer Register* and Biographical Files, *Arguello*, San Diego Historical Society.]

Dogs were a part of California's early ranchos and most settlements. Incessant barking and fighting was tolerated because they served as guardians, ate table scraps and by their keen sense of smell and vision, were inviolate to hunters, but usually they were a tattered lot.

August 16.

"Today I passed a very good time. During the forenoon I was in the house all the time, and of course, had a good time with all the girls. At half past four I took Maria Antonia and Refujia to the sea shore and there we walked up and down the beach, we enjoyed the ride very much. This evening after tea, we had a few games of oucha [oucre] and old maid, passed a few hours very pleasantly and when we had finished playing, someone requested that Refujia and Tula sing, but they would not do it in the parlor, they sang a little outside, but not to me. At half past nine this morning a change took place in the atmosphere, it had been very warm, but a terrible south wind rose which brought some rain accompanied by thunder and lightening. At times the thunder lasted thirty to forty seconds. It was a frightful thing to witness. The San Diego River tonight brought a great deal of water."

Sunday, August 17.

"At the house till eleven or twelve when Tula, Refujia and Lola [his cousin, Maria Dolores] with Jose Antonio and myself went to visit another monument at the point of boundary between the U.S. and Mexico. At the side towards the beach [the Pacific] the following inscription is written: 'Initial point of boundary between the U.S. and Mexico, established by the joint commission, 10th, Oct. A.D.—1849 agreeably to the Treaty dated at the city of Guadalupe Hidalgo, Feb. 1, 1848. John B. Weller, U.S. Comm. Andrew B. Gray, U.S. Surveyor.' On the west [east] side of the tomb, that is towards the hills, the following is inscribed: 'North Latitude 32° 31″ 59″ 58″, Longitude 7^h 48^m 21^s West of Greenwich as determined by Major Wm. E. Emory on the part of the U.S. and Jose Salazar Ylarregui on the part of Mexico.' Towards the south is marked: 'La Republica Mexicana' and on the North, 'The United States of America.' After visiting the monument we went to the sea shore and enjoyed a short time viewing the waves. I saw four antelope and deer, we came home soon after. It was very warm when we left the beach. This evening at the parlor I passed quite a lively time with all the girls, especially Tula. I retired to rest at a very late hour. Jose Maria Estudillo [J.M.'s cousin] was here this morning. Mrs. Theresa Bandini arrived from her ranch this afternoon." Mrs. Theresa Bandini was a daughter of Santiago Arguello of Rancho La Tia Juana and the widow of Jose Maria Bandini of Old Town, San Diego.

August 18.

"I was not very diligent in getting up this morning, but I was up in time for breakfast. Today I was all the time at home and passed many moments in the company of my cousins. Today arrived here, A. Forbes, Jose Maria Bandini and Jose Maria Estudillo; yesterday, F. Arguello." "F. Arguello" was Francisco, a son of J.M.'s hostess and her late husband, Don Santiago Emigdio Arguello. Francisco was born at La Punta in late 1839. On February 12, 1863, he married Luz Osuna, who was born on Rancho San Dieguito in 1845. [Biographical files, *Arguello*, San Diego Historical Society.]

"About six o'clock this afternoon we took a walk with such pleasant company, it was far from not being agreeable. On the way, Forbes and myself ran a race, I was the loser, came home and after tea, we had a grand time in the corridor singing and rejoicing was the order of the hour and afterwards we went into the parlor and danced a quadrille and sang many beautiful songs in Spanish and English such as 'La Despedida Melitar,' 'Annie of the Vale,' etc. In fact, I can safely say that it was a long time since I enjoyed an evening so much as the present. We retired to bed about one o'clock. For the first time tonight I saw the comet, but hardly visible. I took a bath this afternoon."

The August 12, 1958 edition of the Oakland *Tribune* contains the following item pertaining to the comet. It reads: "Tuttle's Comet is sending its vivid 'Tears of St. Lawrence' down from the skies tonight and tomorrow from dusk to early morning. The fireworks are in the form of orange and yellow streaks as the fiery masses enter the earth's atmosphere at the rate of 50 miles per hour. The streaks remain luminous from one to fifteen minutes each. First noted in 1862, the comet has made an annual appearance over northern California as a distinctive celestial phenomena."

By 1862, French and American dances were preferred by the younger Californios because each participant could exhibit more grace and spirit. Dana visiting California in 1835 and '36, watched several early Spanish dances and wrote of his disappointment. "The women stood upright, their hands down by their sides, their eyes fixed upon the ground before them, and slided about without any perceptible means of motion; for their feet were invisible, the hem of their dresses forming a circle about them, reaching to the ground. They looked as grave as though they were going through some religious ceremony, their faces as little excited as their limbs. . . ." The Quadrille [R.H. Dana, *op. cit.*, p. 281, 1887 edition] is of French origin and is danced by four couples. Another favorite, although once frowned upon by upper-class Europeans and the early padres, was the waltz. Reputedly, it was introduced to the Californios by Juan Bandini who lived among the socially elite of Mexico City before coming to San Diego.

August 19.

"I awoke this morning a great deal earlier than yesterday, but would have remained in bed longer if it had not been for Jose Maria who came in our room. During the forenoon, I finished the cage I commenced yesterday. The time has passed with me exceedingly fast and wish that I could recall the happy hours I passed in the company of this good and charitable family for the past five days and begin again, but the thought of them, when I pray, shall remain in my memory as if printed with indelible ink. This evening we all united in the parlor, and played games and sang till eleven o'clock, and when retiring, some remedy was given me for my foot that had been hurt the other day by the stage running over it."

August 20.

"Wrote a letter to Miguel Pedrorena and sent it by Jose Maria Estudillo who arrived here today." Miguel was the only son of Don Miguel Telesforo de Pedrorena, a well-educated native of Castile, Spain. After a few years in Peru, Don Pedrorena journeyed to Santa Barbara where on May 4, 1842, he married Maria Antonia, then not quite sixteen years of age and a daughter of Don Jose Antonio Estudillo. Witnesses were Don Jose Antonio Aguirre and his first wife, Maria Francisca, a sister of the bride. [Santa Barbara Mission Marriage Records, Vol. II, Entry No. 256, May 4, 1842.]

1844 found the Pedrorenas living near the Estudillos in San Diego where on November 10 of the same year, Dona Maria Antonia gave birth to their first child, Miguel. Because the infant was not expected to live, he was baptized on the day of his birth in the small chapel of Casa de Estudillo by his maternal grandfather, Don Jose Antonio Estudillo. One week later, on November 17, 1844, the tiny bundle of humanity was taken to the chapel of the San Diego Presidio to be rebaptized and named Miguel Antonio Francisco by Fr. Vicente R. Olivia. [Mission San Diego Baptismal Records, Vol. II, Entry No. 7075, November 17, 1844.]

During the war with Mexico, Don Miguel Telesforo de Pedrorena served as a captain in the U.S. forces. On July 26, 1846, while the Stars and Stripes were being raised in the plaza opposite Casa de Estudillo, his wife gave birth to their daughter, Ysabel. [Biographical files, *Pedrorena*, Colton Hall, Monterey, California.] In the following year, (1847), Don Miguel Telesforo de Pedrorena was chosen as a delegate to the Constitutional Convention in Monterey and later appointed customs collector of San Diego by Commodore Stockton.

Young Miguel and J.M. were of the same age but our diarist lacked the physical stamina, self-confidence, and the aggressiveness of Miguel who became the social leader of the Southland's younger Californios. Miguel's life was indeed colorful, however of short duration for he died at the age of thirty-eight on Rancho El Cajon which he and his sisters Ysabel, Victoria and Elena had inherited upon the death of their father.

"This morning I commenced to get ready for my trip to Los Angeles by steamer which is expected in this port [San Diego] tomorrow. At half past four or five P.M., Pancho Arguello and myself left for San Diego."

"At my departure many tears were shed by my beloved aunts and cousins, but I consoled them with a promise of return. At San Diego we stopped at Mrs. Johnston's house. The stage arrived about half past eight in the evening and soon I started to the express office and waited a while, but seeing that it took so long to distribute all the letters, I went to the post office and here I waited in great anxiety till the letters were given out; but what was my misfortune, that I did not receive a single letter. From the post office I went back to the express where I inquired for letters and my usual luck happened again, there was nothing for me. I tried my best to get a newspaper, but it was impossible. Pancho and myself went home (Mrs. Johnston's) after this and you can imagine how displeased I was with Lola and my mother for their negligence. I learned from the stage driver that the steamer had arrived at San Pedro and was not coming to San Diego and I lost all hopes of leaving on this steamer and had to console myself with the hope of leaving on this steamer that leaves here the beginning of Septmber."

August 21.

"I was awakened this morning about five A.M. and laid in bed till half past seven without going to sleep. After breakfast, I went to the Cosmopolitan Hotel and commenced reading the account of the burning of the Golden Gate, but did not finish."

On July 27, 1862, the luxury steamer *Golden Gate* left San Francisco for the East coast. Six days later, when but a short distance off the coast of Mexico, a tragic conflagration enveloped the vessel. As the fire was discovered the steamer made for shore at full speed, but the flames made terrifying progress. Although the vessel reached the Mexican shore, it continued to burn to complete destruction. About 338 passengers were aboard when the *Golden Gate* left San Francisco, of whom 223 perished in the flames or by drowning. Also lost was $1,400,000 in the vessel's vaults. [*Alta, California,* August 12, 1862.] W.H. Brewer was in San Francisco on August 10, 1862 and wrote that the city was in great excitement and mourning. "Everyone has lost friends and acquaintances by that accident." [W.H. Brewer, *op. cit.,* p. 294.]

"Went back to the house and commenced to write letters. I wrote a very long one to Lola and another to Juan about the same length, just as I was finishing, Miguel Pedrorena arrived, he came all the way from El Cajon to see me before leaving for San Francisco. As soon as I finished my letters, we went together to visit Mrs. Concepcion Pedleton (Pendleton), but we had hardly been there ten minutes when Pancho arrived in the express wagon ready to go. I went to town and left at the Post Office and we started for La Punta. We had ladies in the wagon, Con. [Concepcion] Machado and her mother who came all the way to the Point with us, on the way a young man by the name of Yorbas met us and he had a watermelon that we soon ate under a willow tree. [The "young man by the name of Yorbas" was undoubtedly a member of the early Yorba family of Los Angeles or San Juan Capistrano.] Arrived at the Ranch about four o'clock and all were very glad that the steamer would not come and in fact, it did not come."

August 22.

"It will be remembered by me that today I kept the Friday as I was accustomed to do it at the College, that is without eating meat, it is worth noticing for on a ranch it is not easy to pass a day without eating meat."

J.M. continues: "I was kept a prisoner during the afternoon for some time in Tula's room. Maria Antonia made me some remedy for my foot and I had to remain in bed till I felt better. I passed the time very pleasantly during the day and especially this evening, about six p.m. when I took a walk and in the parlor with Tula. I enjoyed her company till I retired to bed with the wishes of pleasant dreams. Dona Guadalupe [his aunt] told me of a circumstance that took place between Jose Antonio Estudillo and Dona Victoria soon after they were married and that she acted once a very [bad] part in taring [*sic*] a sash that a lady had made for him before he married Victoria and that when my mother and father came to San Diego the Arguello family paid more care to my mother and father than to the family of Victoria and ever since a spirit of jelousy [*sic*] that part of the family has kept towards us."

The "Sash" was a cummerbund worn tightly about the waist by upper-class Californios. Worn in place of suspenders or belts, they were usually made of vivid satin and fringed at both ends. Perfectly proper it was for a senorita to present a cummerbund to a young unmarried man as a token of friendship and admiration. Gifts, however, often caused comment among friends of both parties. It was not uncommon for a senorita to flush with jealousy and anger upon seeing an admired acquaintance wearing a beautiful cummerbund that had been made by a known or unknown rival.

August 23.

"After breakfast Jose Antonio got the express wagon to go to Las Tinas, and Tula and Dona Maria Antonia, myself and uncle started. After an hour and half of traveling we arrived at the place of destination, nothing worthy of note took place on the way, only we enjoyed the ride as a matter of course, and plagued Tula on the way [about] her beaux and of the Lieutenants of New Town. At the place where we stopped we ate many watermelons and mushmelons, the house was but a shanty of logs. Coming back, we brought many water melons and mushmelons, green corn and other vegetables. On the way we met A. Forbes and Ignatius Arguello and Jose Maria Bandini, and they came back and Tula and Jose went with them. This evening I danced a waltz and a sha–[schottische] with Refujia and the consequence was that I hurt my foot again and could not dance longer. We went to bed at half past eleven or still later. Forbes and I. Arguello remained here for the night and one of their wagon horses went away, so their trip to La Tia Juana tomorrow will be arranged different from the first plan."

Sunday, August 24.

"I had the greatest wish of going to church today that I ever had for a long while, being already three weeks since I heard Mass last; but I could not go to San Diego as there was no conveyance to go. Dona Guadalupe, Refujia and Dolores went to La Tia Juana in the wagon with oxen and left Tula and Maria Antonia at home and about two o'clock, Mr. Couts and Captain Wilcock [Wilcox] arrived at the house and when Forbes heard of their arrival, he left the house and did not come back till they had gone away. They dined with us, had champagne which they brought. About half past four P.M. they went away and took Maria Antonia and Tula with them as they were leaving, Jose Maria Bandini arrived and brought a mule for the wagon for Forbes and at five o'clock, I was left alone in the house with mia tia [my aunt] Pachita and the servant girls. ["Pachita" may have been the diarist's ailing aunt, Maria Magdalena Estudillo.] I felt so lonesome that I went to Tula's room and took a nap till half past eight when I was awoke by my uncle. I took tea and went to write in my journal. Tonight I slept in Guadalupe's room. This morning was very foggy and a western wind blew for the most past of the forenoon."

August 25.

"Before putting anything of what transpired today, it would be very appropriate to remind myself that this is the 25th of August, and this, that today the College opens again and the vacations of 1862 are ended and I find myself six or seven thousand miles from home and no way of getting to the College till the steamer comes. This morning before breakfast I took a gun and went out and shot two hares, the morning was very foggy and cold. I read a good deal during the forenoon—'el Dicciorian

[Diccionario] Manuel and la Fabuld', I suppose I would not have read Spanish if it was not that I was so lonesome. Dona Guadalupe arrived from La Tia Juana. I passed the time very agreeably with Refujia. In our walk this afternoon we saw a nest of a tarantula and could not find the tarantula. I dug a good deal for it. This evening I went to bed earlier than usual. Forbes gave me two letters to deliver."

August 26.

"Today we had visitors from San Diego and New Town; the family of Mrs. Johnston and Lieutenants Smith and Glasby from New Town; they remained till half past five, they took dinner [noon] with us. I was invited to stop tomorrow at the town to see the barracks, I promised to do so."

In 1862, about 4000 Union troops were camped in New Town San Diego. B.I. Hayes was there at the time and wrote: "At new San Diego is stationed Company D. 5th Infantry; payday and its consequences—the guard, Lt. Smith, Lt. Glasby, Lt. French." The post, then known as the *San Diego Barracks* was established in 1846, mainly as a supply depot for towns on the frontier. It was reduced considerably after the war with Mexico. By 1867, the troops and officers had left the area; presently in the midst of San Diego's extensive industrial district.

"This evening whilst looking for a likeness of the deceased Johnny Ward, I found the books where the dates when born of the family of my aunt, and looking over it, I found that Tula (or Maria Gertrudis) and Refujia told me a story. Tula said she was twenty and Refujia was eighteen. Now that is not so, for Tula was twenty-two and going on to twenty-three, born, July 8, 1840 and Refujia was going on twenty-one. When I found this out, Refujia laughed a good deal, as also did I. As soon as I shall see Tula I have something to plague her."

During the day, J.M. packed his personal belongings and arranged for his departure. He was now anxious to leave La Punta but only because he had sorely neglected his religious obligations and was missing classes at Santa Clara College. The deeply religious diarist grieved for his beloved relatives at La Punta because they failed to observe abstinence and faithful Mass; so unlike the northern Arguellos and his own family.

13

Homeward Bound

Old Town—San Diego: August 27, 1862.

"Received a letter this morning from my mother and one from Guadalupe Arguello. At La Punta to five o'clock this afternoon when I left on my way to Los Angeles. Pancho, Dona Pachita & Refugio accompanied me. We stopped at Mrs. Johnson's house. Pancho Estudillo remained at San Diego to make the acquaintance of a new cousin. I met Mrs. Pedleton and Mrs. Aguirre at Mrs. Johnson's house and went home with them to bring a letter from my mother. Came home about eleven o'clock. Tonight I read the *Alta* of the 15th instant and of a later date. This evening I could not go to sleep whilst in bed for a long time on account of the bed, which was not a very good one and consequently I passed a very bad night. In my letter [from his mother] I am told that my sister [Lola] and Joaquinito are very sick; at the receipt of these news I felt very uneasy about them."

August 28.

"I was up this morning at five A.M., got ready to go to Guajomito but the ladies were not ready, had to wait till seven o'clock when we left San Diego; this morning was very clouded and foggy and remained so till ten o'clock when a hot sun appeared and I felt very bad till we got to San Dieguito, that was a quarter passed [*sic*] eleven. At this place we took dinner and a very good one for the occasion. I saw two young ladies, sisters, Miss Lucy and _____."

J.M. and his companions left the hospitable Osunas at two o'clock and ". . . traveled through a very rugged and broken country before getting to

Guajomita. . . ." Enroute they stopped at the Milpitas Rancho comprised of about 1200 acres a few miles southeast of San Luis Rey. Prior to secularization, Rancho Los Milpitas belonged to Mission San Luis Rey de Francia. By 1862, it was known as *Buena Vista* and owned by Cave Johnson Couts. The present town of Vista in San Diego County boasts one of the world's largest packing plants. A great portion of the one-time rancho, which was mainly the grazing lands of the Californios, is a magnificent expanse of citrus and avocado groves and other agricultural products.

From there, they traveled through Rancho Guajomito which adjoined Rancho Guajome where they remained as guests of Mr. Cave Johnson Couts and his charming wife, the former Ysidora Bandini. Mr. Cave Johnson Couts, born on October 11, 1821, was a nephew of Mr. Cave Johnson of Tennessee, who in 1845, served as Postmaster General under President James K. Polk. Cave Johnson Couts was a cultured and well-educated person which is attested by a beautifully written letter he addressed to the Honorable J.R. Poinsette, Secretary of War under President Martin Van Buren. It was written in Alexandria, D.C. on March 11, 1838 and read in part: "I have the honor to receive your communication of the 7th instant, notifying me that the President of the United States has on that day, conditionally appointed me as a cadet in the service of the United States, and that on repairing to West Point in the State of New York between the 1st and 25th of June 1838 and reporting myself to the superintendent of the Military Academy." Mr. Couts closed the letter with: "I have the Honor to be Very Respectfully your Obt. Sevt. Cave Johnson Couts." [Copy of Mr. Cave Johnson Couts' letter and other data pertaining to him, courtesy of the *Records of the Office of the Adjutant General. Military Application Papers, 1837,* National Archives and Records Service, Early Wars Branch, General Services Administration, Washington, D.C.]

Mr. Couts is supposed to have been related to General U.S. Grant. However, his name does not appear on the list of his relatives which was sent to West Point prior to his entrance examination. Couts arrived at West Point in June, 1838, and was graduated from the academy in 1843. After serving on the frontier during the Mexican War, he was stationed in California. He resigned his commission in 1851, shortly before his marriage to Senorita Ysidora Bandini. [W.D. Frazier, *Oceanside—The Gateway to all San Diego County,* p. 2.] Cave Johnson Couts died in 1874 at the age of fifty-three, after which his widow continued to manage the rancho for a few years when it was transferred to other owners. In 1885, Ysidora Bandini de Couts wrote that her property embraced over 2000 acres on which she had resided since 1856. Although it was excellent agricultural land, her attention was given mainly to the raising of cattle and horses. [Ibid, p. 92.]

Rancho Guajome was the largest of the Couts' holding and lay about 2 miles south of Mission San Luis Rey. The acreage derived its name from the Luiseño Indian word "Guajome" meaning "Home of the Frogs." On page 684, *Handbook of the Indians of California,* Krober states that the Luiseño Indians, having no tribal name of their own, were named *Luiseños* after Mission San Luis Rey De Francia. Upon secularization, the mission's properties were distributed among the neophytes, but their acreage was soon purchased from them for a pittance and by 1846, scarcely an acre of ground was left to the Indians.

The scenic expanse was held by two former neophytes until about 1850 when it was purchased by Abel Stearns who presented it to his sister-in-law, Ysidora Bandini, upon her marriage to Cave Johnson Couts April 5, 1851. Mr. and Mrs. Couts were then living in San Diego, but about five years later, they removed to Rancho Guajome and established a magnificent hacienda. It was indeed a home of beauty, unexcelled hospitality and gracious living. At present, the former Couts' *hacienda* and surroundings is as enchanting as it was in 1862. Mrs. Couts was the diarist's cousin and a daughter of Don Juan Bandini and his first wife, Maria de los Dolores Damiana Estudillo, whom he married in 1822.

August 29.

"I was up this morning at six A.M. when Refujia got ready and we took a walk in the garden and then came to breakfast. I wrote a letter to my mother, because I expected to remain at this place till the arrival of the next stage; but I changed my mind and came away. Came to Mr. Thibit's [Tibbett's change-station] with Mr. Couts, here I took the stage for Los Angeles and left after dinner which was about half past one. We started with four horses and did not change till we came to San Juan Capistrano; there were five passengers in the stage. Came to the San Mateo Ranch at the mouth of the beach road, about half past five or six and this time we did not get out of the stage. About eight o'clock we arrived at San Juan Capistrano. I stopped at Mr. Forster's house. Ramon Arguello came with me as far as the Coyotes Ranch." [Don Jose Ramon Arguello was a son of Don Santiago Arguello of Rancha La Tia Juana. On February 9, 1834, he married Maria Feliciana Pico, a sister of Andres and Pio Pico.] [Biographical Files, *Arguello,* San Diego Historical Society.]

"This morning Tula Arguello gave me a pink boquet with a small piece of lemon verbena. I had already given her a small boquet." [*sic*]

August 30.

"I was called up by the stage driver this morning at half past two or three o'clock A.M. and went to the stage station [Garcia House] where I took breakfast and left San Juan about four A.M. The morning was foggy, but it cleared off when the sun showed its shining rays. We traveled at a fast rate till we got to Los Coyotes Ranch bordering Orange County about 20 miles from Los Angeles. We had already stopped at Anaheim and changed horses and bought some grapes and ate them on the way, and from here we drove slow. On the way I saw thousands of rabitts [*sic*], hares, etc. We arrived at Los Angeles at half past one P.M. and I made my way to the house [Daltons'] to see the family. My heart beat with joy to find Lola already a great deal better from her sickness and also Joaquinito was doing well, fast recovering from his last illness."

Sunday, August 31.

"This morning I got ready to go to church and went to ten o'clock Mass, had two sermons, one in English and one in Spanish. This afternoon I visited the house of the Misses Olveras and Dolores played the harp magnificently. I went with George Dalton and coming we stopped at another family's house. The afternoon was rather dull for me, this evening in the parlor we played at cards and enjoyed a short time very well."

September 2.

". . . About half past nine or ten o'clock A.M. the stages arrived from the boat at San Pedro. I received one hundred and sixty dollars sent by Juan, two letters and a bundle I got out of the express, and tomorrow I expect the freight that comes for my mother. A great crowd arrived in the steamer, most of them miners. We had some visits this afternoon of Mrs. Dolores Sepulveda and Refujia Bandini [Juan Bandini's second wife] and another lady."

The first discovery of gold in California took place in March 1842, about thirty-five miles north of Los Angeles, formerly the property of Mission San Fernando. After a few years of rewarding efforts, the shortage of water forced the amateur miners to abandon the area. By 1862, another rush had developed in the vicinity of Santa Anita, San Gabriel, and in the San Fernando districts. When enterprising Phineas Banning of San Pedro noted that throngs were plaguing every merchant in Los Angeles for pans, shovels or any tool to retrieve the monetary metal, he returned to his San Pedro warehouse, loaded his wagon with an assortment of supplies, and drove directly to the mining areas. Before he and his horses had time to rest, every item was sold, while others appealed for another delivery. [M. Krythe, *op. cit.*, pp. 112-113.]

R.H. Dana, Jr., who returned from Los Angeles in 1859, wrote that it was a flourishing town of about twenty-thousand inhabitants with brick sidewalks and blocks of stone or brick houses.

September 3.

". . . This evening we had a party at the house, given by Mr. George Dalton, we danced till four o'clock in the morning, we had five musicians playing. I enjoyed the time very well. I danced most of the time with the Arguellos of Los Angeles. I retired to rest about five o'clock."

September 5.

"Wrote a letter this morning to Mr. Couts. . . . I was obliged to get up this morning at half past six on account of the stage leaves Los Angeles this morning at eight. At seven A.M., Bob and myself had breakfast at the Bella Union Hotel. At quarter after eight I bid my family and all the household a long farewell and then took the stage to San Pedro where we arrived about twelve." In the back of *Journal for 1862,* J.M. wrote he had received $40.00 from his mother and "Passage to San Francisco—$27.50."

"On our way to San Pedro a person on horseback came up to the stage, and at his request, the stage stopped and the individual handed a summons to appear for something, for what I did not inquire; but the fact was, that this summons was for George Dalton and this person on horseback insisted that I was George Dalton, it was a long time before I could persuade him that my name was Estudillo and not for whom he wished to take me."

On Sunday, May 20, 1860, B.I. Hayes wrote: "All San Diego is in a ferment. H. Dalton, convicted yesterday of grand larceny in the court of Sessions, escaped last night from the cage of iron that constitutes the county jail." Dalton was captured near San Luis Rey two days later, when ". . . the court met and in the excitement, sentenced him to imprisonment for twelve years. The prisoner is quite a young man of handsome address; he sent for law books and defended his own case. . . ." [B.I. Hayes, *Pioneer Notes—1815-1877*, pp. 204, 205.] Because the culprit was "quite a young man of handsome address," one is apt to wonder if he was Henry, and not the George Dalton J.M. wrote of, son of the wealthy and prominent Henry Dalton.

"We left San Pedro at two o'clock. At half past ten we arrived at Santa Barbara, landed the freight and came away at two o'clock A.M. I was not up, I remained in bed."

September 6.
"Up at half past six, had breakfast and went on deck, at the time it was very foggy, quite a number of whales were to be seen in the bay. Anchored at San Luis Obispo at half past nine, went through thick fog and there was danger striking against some of the rocks that were close where we anchored, and for that reason the steamer went very slow for a half an hour."

During March, April, and May, immense whales were exceedingly prevalent from Monterey southward. Brewer wrote in May 1861 that the number of whale bones on the sandy Monterey beach was astonishing and in the previous year, one had been caught which was ninety-three feet long and that over a hundred barrels of oil were extracted from the mammal. [W.H. Brewer, *op. cit.*, p. 184.] During the whale season it was deemed extremely hazardous to be on the ocean in a small craft, especially between San Diego and San Pedro.

Sunday, September 7.
"I was up this morning at half past six or seven and dense fog was at the time, so that the steamer had to stop for a while lest she might strike a rock; but at twenty after seven I saw the Heads and at the same time, Telegraph Hill, and soon we entered the Golden Gate and at eight we landed."

"The Heads" are the high and almost barren cliffs at the entrance of the Golden Gate Strait, named by the noted pathfinder, John Charles Fremont. [J.P. Young, *op. cit.*, Vol. 1, p. 122.] San Francisco's unique Telegraph Hill was first known as Loma Alta. It was of little importance until the fall of 1849, when a structure was erected on the promontory which resembled a windmill with arms indicating the type of vessel entering the strait and San Francisco Bay. Later, when the semaphore-system was displaced by telegraph, the historical landmark become known as "Telegraph Hill."

September 10.

"I wrote two letters today, one to my mother, the other to Lola. Today it was very warm and I waited till afternoon to go to see the copper mine in the hills which I found to my own knowledge that it was very rich. I got a stone from another place and there seems to be something else in this stone. I brought some specimens to take to Santa Clara with me. I drove Mr. Ward's mare. I had tea with Vicente and both of us went to the place where the mine lay."

In September, 1862, W.H. Brewer and his associates studied various small mines in the eastern foothills between Oakland and San Jose. During their surveys, they set up a temporary camp in the vicinity of Hayward. Brewer wrote: ". . . Wednesday, I visited some of the hills in the neighborhood, among the rest a 'coal mine' where much money has been expended and not a particle of coal found, and where geological knowledge would have saved the money. Then a 'copper mine' just as bad and more expensive. I went down a shaft a hundred feet, hanging on a rope, then into a drift in rock where it is impossible for a mine to occur—money thrown away. I told the man to stop digging, and I think he will after sinking a few more hundreds." [W.H. Brewer, *op. cit.,* p. 184.] The miner may have been J.M.'s aggressive, twenty-nine year old brother, Juan Vicente. Several others had reported finding various minerals in the general vicinity. One was a coal-ledge found on June 18, 1862 on the premises of W.O. Harris near Warm Springs; about six miles south of Mission San Jose. [W. Hally, *op. cit.,* p. 164.]

On September 11th, J.M. sent several small items to his mother and Lola, made a few calls, and enjoyed supper with Mr. and Mrs. Abel Stearns at the Russ House in San Francisco. After supper he met Juan Alvarado and the two called upon Salvador Vallejo at the Metropolitan Hotel where they met a Mr. Estrada. Vallejo was born in Monterey on January 1, 1813 and was a brother of General M.G. Vallejo. Two days later, he was baptized *Jose Manuel y Salvador.* [Carmel Mission Baptismal Records, Book 1, Entry 1865, January 3, 1813.] In 1862, he with his wife and five children were living on a small portion of his one-time vast estate in Napa County.

Vallejo's guest was probably Don Joaquin Estrada, who resided on his

Atascadero Rancho, located about twenty-two miles north of San Luis Obispo. By 1862, this scenic expanse was the last of his vast holdings; having sold or lost other properties to squatters. The Vallejos and Estradas at one time maintained *haciendas* which were princely estates not entirely dependent upon the raising of cattle. Don Jose Manuel Salvador Vallejo died in 1876, a discouraged and comparatively poor man.

Don Alvarado may have been in San Francisco to attend to legal matters in relation to his holdings. During the squatter problems of the 1850s and '60s, he lost thousands of acres and a large portion of his wealth through costly litigations. 1862 was the beginning of a serious, three-year drought during which he, Stearns, the Estradas and many others lost a fortune in cattle, sheep and horses.

September 16.

"At home all day and arranged Mr. Ward's writing desk, put all the accounts, letters, deeds, etc. in their proper places. [Note to effect he studied this at Santa Clara.] I saw in the accounts for the family with the hotel [Estudillo House], that my board was fifty dollars, now that seemed too much for the time I boarded at the house. I made up my mind to go with Mr. Ward tomorrow to Pinole and see Luis' race. I got Mr. Crane's riding saddle. All my expectations for my trip were put to an end this evening when Mr. Ward came from the city, for I was told to take two men tomorrow up to the copper vein, and there was my trip."

September 17.

". . . took the two men to the copper vein and then came back, got ready to go to Pinole. I left San Leandro at half past eight on horseback, traveled very fast till the other side of 'Cerrito,' I caught up with Jose Jesus Peralta, we went together, got to Pinole at half past eleven. The race came off at three P.M. I saw Luis, all the family of Jose Martinez, also Carlotta Castro. The race came off at four which resulted in favor of Luis, the stallion winning the race by five or six yards. I went to Jose Martinez' house this evening and passed a miserable night, very little clothes on the bed."

The distance from San Leandro to Pinole by way of El Cerrito de San Antonio measured between twenty-five and thirty miles. Unless J.M. bypassed the San Pablo road, forcing such speed upon his horse in the heat of September is an example of cruelty to horses, practiced my many of the Californios although in most cases, it was not intentional.

Tales of mistreatment of animals by the Californios and others occasionally reached the eastern states. The September, 1855, issue of Boston's *Ballou Pictorial* magazine bears the following account. "Two brutes lately raced their steed from Auburn, Cal. to Sacramento and back, 77 miles. The one, a mule, was dragged and beaten by several men during the last 15 miles. The horse either died or was abandoned on the road." During the Spanish and Mexican periods in California, horses were so plentiful that when one was rented, owners were rarely concerned about the steeds, but insisted that the spurs and saddles be returned.

R.H. Dana, Jr. witnessed this while in Monterey and wrote: "When they wish to show their activity, they made no use of their stirrups in mounting, but striking the horse, spring into the saddle as he starts and sticking their long spurs into him, go off on a full run. Their spurs are cruel things, having four or five rowels an inch in length, dull and rusty. The flanks of horses are often sore from them, and I have seen men coming in from chasing bullock with their horses' hind legs and quarters covered with blood." [R.H. Dana, Jr., *op cit.*, p. 56, 1840 edition.]

September 18.

"Went to Rancho San Joaquin, passed by the old Pinole, stopped at Dr. Tennent's, had breakfast and left for the Ranch where I arrived about twelve o'clock; it was very warm at the time and especially about two o'clock. I saw Frank and spoke to him about the object of my visit, for the rent of Manuel and O'Neil, he said he had no money, that Manuel would have some next week. I took a short nap and then saddled 'El Limon' and rode to Manuel's. I saw there Rafaela [his aunt, Mrs. Samuel Tennent] and coming home I stopped at O'Neils. I was invited to take supper with them which I did. Came home late in the evening. Jose Antonio arrived this evening, quite harsh words passed between Jose Antonio and Frank Ward."

September 19.

"Up pretty early, caught my horse to ride to San Leandro but before leaving, I went to the beach [San Pablo Bay]. I came to Mr. Tennent's house and from there I came to Pinole where I saw Luis Martinez and then came to San Pablo. I went to see the Misses Castros. Gave my photograph to Carlotta, she of course asked for it. I passed quite a pleasant time with them. J. Peralta came with me from San Pablo; we traveled at a very slow rate and arrived at San Leandro at seven. I went to Vicente's [J.M.'s brother] house immediately, I saw there his brother-in-law, Henry Dalton, who arrived from Los Angeles today. I had supper with them, then came home and it was very dark, the horse fell with me on the road once, and going by the fence, a rail caught my pants and tore my pants and would have hurt my leg had it not been for the leg of my boot. Passing the Seminary at Oakland, I saw Fannie Willis who came out of the gate and would have spoken to me if I had interrogated her first. Received a letter from Lola and a military sword, they were sent to Vicente's." J.M.'s brother, Jose Vicente, married Eulalia Zamorano on September 1, 1861.

During the Victorian period, it was considered improper for a well-bred young lady to greet a young man unless he had bowed politely and addressed her in a formal manner. She was never to exhibit frivolity or obvious interest in his presence. If a young lady was a student of a private institution, she was not to step beyond its gates unless accompanied by a member of the faculty or a visiting relative.

September 20.

"At San Leandro all afternoon. I went to Oakland on horseback, rode in twenty-five minutes, I had business of importance. I wrote a letter to Frank Ward and left it at Shattuck's stable, to be taken to San Joaquin by Jose Antonio." In 1862, the *Shattuck & Hillegas Livery Stable* was located on Broadway, between 7th and 8th Streets in Oakland. It was first established on the east side of Broadway between Front and First Streets by William Hillegas and Francis K. Shattuck, who were among the first squatters on Domingo Peralta's portion of Rancho San Antonio.

"This afternoon I went to Peralta's house and ate many peaches in the orchard. This evening Mr. English, Mr. Smith and myself, whilst we were taking a walk, stopped at John Brady's house, at this time a party was going on, there were three ladies from the city, we danced till ten o'clock. I made the acquaintance of a young lady, Miss Burns, there was a very rough crowd. When I came to my room I made up my mind to go to confession tomorrow."

No doubt the diarist returned ashamed of his behavior at the party, either because he had partaken of more wine than he was accustomed to, or had taken liberties with the ladies of "the very rough crowd." It remained doubtful however, if his transgression was more than relaxed deportment. He hurried to confession after having attended a theatrical performance which he deemed exceedingly improper. This was in Virginia City, where J.M. was obliged to care for his brother-in-law, Mr. John Nugent, who had developed a serious infection, confining him to his bed for about two weeks. During this period, J.M. read glowing accounts of the play "Mazeppa" in the city's *Territorial Enterprise* and overheard startling comments as he wandered about the settlement. Unknown to his sister or Mr. Nugent, J.M. purchased a ticket at Maguire's Opera House, but sheepishly requested a seat in the back row and near the doorway in fear of being seen by one of Mr. Nugent's friends. Before the last curtain had lowered, he dashed out of the theater and returned to the hotel by way of dark alleys. He later wrote he attended the performance merely out of curiosity.

"I had heard so much of it that I proposed to go and see it with my own eyes. Well! What did I see? A woman in tights on the back of a horse, and let loose on the stage." That the diarist rushed to confession on the following morning is understandable because Mark Twain vented his opinion of the performance only in part when he wrote: "Let a pure youth witness Mazeppa once and he is pure no longer."

On September 22, our diarist picked two large boxes of apples to be sent to his relatives. Two days later, he prepared three more boxes of apples for the same purpose. These were from Mr. Edmondson's orchards at the base of the foothills about one-half mile northeast of San Leandro Creek. On September 3rd, J.M. accompanied Vicente to the Pacific Wharf in San Francisco. As Vicente was boarding the "Brother Jonathan," J.M. saw his friend, Alfredo Bandini, who was also leaving for Los Angeles. He had been boarding at Santa Clara College, but owing to illness, was obliged to return home. Alfredo, Juan de la Cruz, and Arturo Bandini were the sons of Don Juan Bandini and his second wife, Refugia Arguello. Some time after Don Juan Bandini's death in 1859, his widow and her sons left San Diego to reside in Los Angeles.

Vicente left to be with his wife, Eulalia Zamorano, who had remained in Los Angeles as a guest of the Daltons.

September 28.

". . . Mr. Ward left this afternoon for Warm Springs on his way to Santa Clara, I promised to start tomorrow. This evening I was present at the singing school, they sang three or four patriotic aires, the female voices deserved a great deal of credit, but as for the chorus of males, it resembles the bowling [*sic*] of oxen, of course with the exception of Mr. Ham, the teacher, who deserves all merit; at quarter after nine everything was over. I came home and brought Sophia Ward with me. Sometime before going to bed I read to Magdalena some pieces from the 'American speaker.'"

The fall session of Santa Clara College opened on August 25th. Mr. Ward must have journeyed to the institution to explain the reason for J.M.'s absence which was attributed to Juana Estudillo's financial difficulties. Students who left the college for Christmas or summer vacations and failed to return on the opening day of a session were, by the fact of their absence, excluded until the following session; except in cases where the parents or guardian of the dilatory student could give a reason satisfactory to the president.

September 29.

"The sun brightened this morning as if it awaited some great spectacle to take place, and so it did happen, for we see at half-past twelve or one o'clock P.M., a gathering of people under the trees in front of the hotel. This was a grand mass meeting of the citizens of the county to raise funds for the relief of the wounded soldiers of the army and navy of the North. The Rev. Starr King, Ed. Tompkins, Fred Beelings from the city addressed the meeting. San Leandro presented quite a lively appearance, quite a large number of people were present, of course many ladies. The contributions were over four thousand dollars. All passed over very well, but one or two cases of noisy drunkers. About half past six or seven, San Leandro presented her usual quietness. There was no ball as it had been anticipated by some. I forgot to say that the speakers brought their aires with them. The boys from the Oakland College came in the stage; they acted very wildly."

During the evening of the 29th, J.M. prepared his clothing and books in preparation of leaving for Santa Clara on the following morning. Although he was anxious to return, his sensitive nature and pride prompted him to wonder if his class-mates knew or suspected the reason for his tardiness.

14

The Fall Session at Santa Clara College

September 30.

"At half past ten today I left on the stage to the College. Mr. Ward arrived from the Springs before I left, did not bring the money for the College. I was told that it would be sent in two or three days. I rode on top of the stage as far as Alvarado, from there to the Mission [San Jose] I rode inside, it was very dusty. I went to see Ed Palmer and he invited me to stay till tomorrow, though I thanked him that I could not, he pressed me so much that I had to remain. We went to Warm Springs, played four games of Shovel [shuffle?] board. I beat him one and he beat me three. I paid for the drinks and he for the cigars. This evening we played eight games of Oucho [Oucre]. Obed Palmer was at the Mission."

W.H. Brewer who took the same route in June 1861 wrote: "While seated on the stage we often could not see the leaders [the first two horses] at all for the dust. The driver said the dust often becomes so fine, and eight inches deep, before the close of the dry season, filling the air with dust clouds." [W.H. Brewer, *op. cit.*, p. 121.]

"Up this morning at quarter to nine, I slept with Edward last night and he was very lazy in getting up. After breakfast we went to the Mission, we were at E.L. Beard's orchard, came home [Palmer's] and made a target to shoot at with the rifles and we shot eight or nine shots. I hit the bull's eye once and the rest of the shots around it with the exception of one which missed the target entirely. We went to the Springs and had some other games of shoving, I was beaten again, went home [Palmer's] and had lunch after which the stage came by and we ran to catch up. [On October 1, J.M. rode in the omnibus (from San Jose) to Santa Clara.] I arrived at the College a little after six. The first thing that attracted my

132

attention was the new building of the Fathers." [The present Faculty Building, not to be confused with the building J.M. saw, was erected in 1911 and parallels the site of the Franciscan Friars' residence which stood near the present Jesuit structure.]

"I saw most of the Fathers this evening and spoke to some of the boys before going to bed."

Mission San Jose was founded in 1797 about twelve miles northeast of San Jose. Prior to secularization, in December 1836 it was one of California's most flourishing Missions. The deterioration was so rapid and complete that by 1862, the chapel, most of the agricultural areas and former gardens presented a pitiful scene of abuse and neglect. Visiting it in 1861, Brewer wrote: "The church is large, gaudily painted in the inside, but dilapidated; the congregation a mixture of Indian, Spanish, mixed breed, Irish, with a few Germans, French, and Americans." Beard's orchard, formerly the property of the Mission, was planted in the early 1860s by E.L. Beard and Henry Ellsworth. Brewer mentioned Warm Springs: "These have quite a reputation for the cure of sundry diseases, and the houses, ground, etc., are better fitted for comfort and luxury than any other mineral springs we have seen here." He added that the sulfur waters were recognized as beneficial by the Indians prior to the arrival of the Mexicans and Spaniards, who named the area Agua Caliente.

The first few days at Santa Clara College were uneventful except for the arrival of a bundle of clothing from his sister, Magdalena Nugent. On the eighth of October, George Hoge arrived to pick up his clothing, trunk, books, and personal items because he, Newman and Francisco Valencia of San Francisco had been expelled from the college because they had left the institution without permission some time during the previous week. The severity of the punishment is probably because they had spent several hours in San Jose or had gone swimming in Guadalupe Creek without approval of the president or other members of the faculty.

George Hoge was a son of Judge and Mrs. J.P. Hoge, who arrived in San Francisco in the late 1850s. Their daughter, Pauline, married Mr. Delphine M. Delmas, one of Santa Clara College's most distinguished graduates. George Hoge later became a prominent attorney in San Francisco.

October 10.

"Wrote a letter to my mother, directed it to San Diego. This morning I was told by Father Caredda that Father Young said I needed more reading and it would be better for me to remain in the same class, and accordingly I followed his advice. I was out in town today to inquire what days that the Overland Mail to Lower California left, they didn't know at the Post Office when it left San Jose, for it did not come to Santa Clara at all; they send the mail from here to San Jose. When I came back to the College, I was in a perfect perspiration and could not study in the study room till I was refreshed. This evening I saw in the *Bulletin* of yesterday, an article taken from the *Contra Costa Gazette* where it said that Kibbiss, the cook at Rancho San Joaquin, had been stabbed by two Americans. At length knives were drawn and the Indian received two blows, one in his breast and one in his abdomen, the latter forcing out his entrails. It is supposed that he can not recover. The two men ran away and in the escape they seized two horses and rode to the town of Martinez. They were caught when just about crossing to Venicia. Their names are said to be Wilson & McCann."

October 11

"This morning in English, I was somewhat displeased with Valenzuela on account of his unruly mode of acting when I was asked a question in grammar, he made all the efforts to answer himself." ["Valenzuela" was either Enrique or Jose, sons of Jose Antonio Valenzuela who resided in San Juan, a small settlement near Mission San Juan Bautista. The community later became known as *San Juan Bautista*.]

October 13.

"Of all my College days, this has been the wretchedest, no peace has dwelled within this troubled bosom in the whole day since grammar class to the hour of writing these few lines, seven o'clock in the evening. I have wished that I would not have had to come back this session and I declare that if I am kept in the same English class after Christmas, I will not come back, at least if the same teacher teaches the class. After the class was over this morning, I took out my grammar to the study room to have Father Young explain something I did not understand, when some three or four boys called him and he commenced to speak to them. They told him some trifles, the fact was, that he left me standing with my book in my hand and did not finish his explanation, the small boys were more important to him; this I considered the worst kind of insult and I hope I shall see the time when I can have an explanation of this act of my teacher. This evening the boys went to the Circus, I did not go because I had too many duties to perform and expected to write to San Diego, this last thing I did not do."

Sunday, October, 19.

"After study this afternoon or rather catechism, we went walking and went on the San Jose Road. Some of the boys had plenty of fruit at an orchard to which they went, but I remained out with some boys. They got the fruit for nothing. As we were about to come away, the President, Rev. B. Villiger, S.J., came up to us, he came from San Jose. When I got home [the college] this afternoon I was very tired and my feet hurt very much. A. Spivalo was here this afternoon, and he said that there were hopes of our getting the long wished-for rifles, as he had been to Sacramento and spoke with General Kibbee."

October 20.

"After supper I went down and sat by myself on the last bench by the corridor of the dormitory and contemplated for a good while what course in life I should follow when out of College. Sometimes I thought or remaining till I would graduate; at others, I thought of not coming any more after this session and if circumstances would not permit, I would not come back after Christmas. For a long while these thoughts were in my mind, they were expelled when Townsend came up to where I was and soon after the bell rang for beads [rosary] and we had to repair thither."

October 21.

"Received this afternoon about half past four o'clock, a telegraphic dispatch from Mr. Ward saying that he will send the money tomorrow. The dispatch was sent from Oakland at twenty-two minutes after twelve. Nothing else of any importance occurred during this day."

October 22.

"This morning I asked Father Caredda to let me go to San Jose this afternoon and he granted me permission. After chemistry class I went to town and took the omnibus, my business at San Jose was to see if Mr. Ward had sent the money by the Oakland Stage. I waited till the stage arrived; but I was disappointed, nothing was sent. I sent by the Oakland stage to Mrs. Ward, the two canaries that Father Caredda gave me. . . . I was told by F. Neri that he wanted me to give a short lecture next Wednesday, on Ebulition before the College. I got a new book from the Library, the Brackbridge Hall."

October 23.

"They let us sleep half an hour longer than usual. At a meeting of the Cadets, Mr. Baker resigned his ensigney, and I was unanimously elected to that office. . . . After supper we went walking, went on the San Jose Road, and passed the bridge at San Jose and went to the railroad bridge and walked home by the railroad track, coming out at the Alameda Road again. Few of the boys walked at a fast rate, I was very tired when I came to the college. I have been very uneasy about the money that Mr. Ward promised to send."

October 24.

"I received this morning a letter from Mr. Ward, brought to me from San Jose by Crandell. I learnt that he had sent two hundred dollars by the stage. I asked Father Caredda's permission to go and bring the money. I got the money from Mr. Crandell. I bought several articles of stationery, a Spanish Dictionary, English and Spanish, paid $6.75, Lord Chesterfield's Letters to his son, sundries, $4.00. I saw in San Jose, James Breen, H. Farley, B. Murphy, we had a game of billiards. Farley was my partner, we beat them. There was great excitement this morning when I came to San Jose, on account of the scape [*sic*] of Felipe, the prisoner who was to have been hung this morning. He killed the jailer and four others made the scape [*sic*]. I came back to Santa Clara about half past eleven."

Had Father Caredda known of the terrifying event and that four desperados were still at large, he most certainly would not have permitted the boys to leave the campus. Reward posters dotted San Jose, Santa Clara and all the roadways, but the criminals were never apprehended. A year later, it was reported that Felipe Hernandez, the most vicious and brutal of the four, had been murdered near the Colorado River.

On October 4, J.M. contributed one dollar towards the purchase of an organ for the Sodality and again encountered difficulties with Father Neri. "I asked him when he was going to give me my lecture back and to my great astonishment, he said he had already given it to Valenzuela because he found many things to insert in mine. I was raging mad to hear this, after he promised it to me, and gave it to somebody else. I thought there must have been something else besides connected with it, not that something was to be inserted in my lecture, why did he not tell it to me before, he had it already when he told me I was to deliver it. I shall see that I have this explained to me. I wrote this evening about a page letter to Miss Mary Gray of El Rancho Puente. I heard that Ed Palmer was going to the Oakland College in a few days." [At that time the college had about 200 students.]

J.M.'s discontent and self-pity mounted by the hour. On the following day he wrote: "I am sorry to say, that every day I am more dissatisfied with my English class, but what could I do, I must submit to remain in it till I pass an examination and this will be, I suppose after Christmas." [Despite his indignation and profound disappointment, J.M.'s breeding prevented him from venting his anger in the presence of the Jesuit instructors.]

October 28.

". . . Our class of Philosophy was very interesting today, on the Pendelum, etc. At bookkeeping class great scenes were enacted this afternoon. Duffy was the hero. Mr. Pascal, a lay teacher, was raging mad—he opened the door once to put him out. In fact the poor old man lost his few patience, and as a matter of course it followed, that the whole class was reported to Father Caredda."

November 1.

"This morning I went to confession. This day being All Saint's Day, it was observed as a holy day, there being high Mass in the big church, I attended it being the first time this session. We had resided [*sic*] the office of the Sodality this morning. Our dinner was better than usual, especially the desserts that they gave us, wine, or meant for it. After dinner a dispute arose between Van Ness and myself also Duffy on my side, for so the question demanded it, on the great subject of Religion. Mr. Van Ness' argument on the scriptures was that what the Protestants thought was from the Scriptures. This I admitted, but it remained to show me if their translation of the sacred volume was the same as the original if the Pro. had not changed anything. The question to which this gentleman did not give an answer was this; I asked him whether the true church existed before Luther's time. The gentleman acknowledged that he was well versed in the scriptures and yet he would not admit many of the arguments that we brought forward, mostly quoted from the Bible he would stand to reason. This evening we had a holy night though after Vespers I went into the study room, I studied awhile."

November 3.

"I received two letters this afternoon, one from Lola and another from Refujio Arguello, both from San Diego. Lola writes with the date of the 24th. This is the first letter to me from that distant country. She expressed a dislike for the place, too lonesome and degraded to live there and expects to come away by the end of December. Asks me to send her a cage, to send me a mocking bird."

Lola's opinion of San Diego was not surprising. An undated notation, under *Memoranda* of his Journal, reads: "Never in the world could I imagine to myself that such a miserable country could exist as the country of San Diego and the town itself, which is not worth the trouble of leaving [living] there, because you will die of hunger, if you do not take a good supply of money to procure the provisions which are there sold at enormous prices. The only thing I found in San Diego to take pleasure in, was the amount of game in which one enjoys himself hunting. Quails, never in my life did I see so many as when I made the trip overland from Los Angeles to San Diego. Rabbits, hares and all sorts of game are abundant. Antelopes and deer I had the chance of seeing at La Punta and San Diego."

November 4th and 5th were uneventful and depressing. The little iron, wood-burning stove was replaced in the study hall as chilly winds and occasional showers visited Santa Clara County. With each gust of wind, yellow leaves from the orchards wafted downward to settle on the thirsty land. Each day found the normally tidy Fathers' yard dotted with the delicate petals of the last Banksia roses and pale yellow leaves from the great wisteria vines that had shaded the lengthy arbor of hand-hewn timbers dating from the Mission Period. Winter was announcing her presence.

Thursday, November 6.

"Reichert and myself got a buggy from Capt. Ham and went to San Jose. It was very foggy when we left Santa Clara. The sun looked to us like the moon. I got my hair cut in San Jose, I also shaved, but not my mustache. I went to visit the Misses Picos. I also saw the three Misses Castros [his cousins from San Pablo] who came on the stage from Alviso. They promised to come and see me on Saturday. We dined at the French

Restaurant. Reichert and myself spoke to Martin Murphy and he told me that he had seen Mr. Ward in the city a few days ago. . . . At Mr. Pico's I saw Mr. Leese, not the young man."

The following day, J.M. waited impatiently for his cousins, the daughter of Victor Castro and his wife, Luisa Martinez, who had promised to visit him. As they did not arrive, he strolled dejectedly about the gardens, attended Vespers, and retired for the night, disappointed, perplexed, and lonesome. Throughout the semester when many other students enjoyed visitors, J.M. remained in the study hall or wandered about the campus with one of the Fathers. Only once during the semester had a letter arrived from his mother and that one was fault-finding. Sunday, the 8th, he again waited for the Castros, ". . . but they did not come and now I am tired of waiting."

November 10.

"I received the *Sacramento Union* of last week this evening. After the usual news, I found many things unknown to me, such as the shock of an earthquake felt at San Leandro. This morning I was told by Luis Arguello's son, Luis L., that there was a lady at Pinedo's home who wished to see me. I sent word out by little Pinedo to tell her to come to the parlor tomorrow. I do not know who she could be. I have lost all hopes of the Misses Castros coming to see me. I heard from Vallejo that Ocha had told him that our copper mine had proof of failure, there was not copper in great quantities."

November 11.

"This morning I heard why Misses Castros had not come to see me, but rather I understood why I did not see them, for on Sunday afternoon they came in a carriage to Santa Clara and inquired for me. I have not heard what answer they gave them at the door."

November 13.

"This day will be long remembered by me. I had what is generally called a good time. Little before dinner, Mrs. Shaffner, Mrs. Aleys with her daughter and Miss Shaffner and Miss Grace Riddle came to visit the College. I went around the College with them and to the hotel also. At the hotel we had lunch and after, retired to the parlor where singing and playing on the piano was the order of the time." [Later in the afternoon, the diarist drove pretty Miss Riddle about Santa Clara in a handsome surrey and was specially delighted when several of his classmates chanced to see him with one of Notre Dame's most popular and charming belles. However, the delightful day ended unhappily when he returned to the college a little after five o'clock when he was informed that the Castro girls had just left after waiting for him an hour or more.]

November 14.

"I heard from Faure & Bowie that a paper of candies with a china image or something like it, but anyhow, that they were introduced into the Convent and directed to Miss Grace Riddle and signed by Bowie. Father Caredda had this morning spoken with Bowie, Faure and I believe Hastings, to find out who was the person that sent this article into the Convent. Of course they directed themselves to Bowie as it was signed by him, but he denied having done such a thing. Whoever did this, indeed, proves to be a black-guided person, for no gentleman would have done such a thing. The picture that was painted was the doing of no gentleman. Father Caredda says that if it is found out that such a thing was done by anybody from this college, that he will be expelled immediately and so he deserves."

November 15.

". . . after the recess, the band played a few tunes as the wind gage with the top pole was raised and fixed on the cupola. There was great rejoicing among the boys, Fathers, and workmen and on the strength of it, the company asked for a holy day which the President granted us. This afternoon for the first time I was in a new building; three other boys and myself with Father Nattini went to the highest point of the building, at least I did. No prettier view could be had of the valley than from this point, we could see very far off. I got permission from Father Caredda to go out this afternoon, soon after dinner I went straight to see my aunt, she desired last Thursday to go to San Jose and visit the Convent and this time I offered to take her, her little daughter and boy went also. I called for Sister Mary and she took us around the Convent, saw all or at least most of the apartments which indeed, are a great many, went as far as the observatory and from there had a good sight of the surrounding country, saw very clearly the cupola of our building. Coming from the playground to the parlor I had an opportunity of seeing Miss G. and the Murphys. As I was going by, she, G.R., in a low voice said, though I heard her distinctly, 'Mr. Estudillo.' I did not turn around, but waited awhile till Sister Mary had passed and then took off my hat and bowed. I saw one of the Vallejos, now a Sister [and a daughter of Jose Jesus Vallejo, who was born at Monterey in 1798]. We came back to Santa Clara at five. I was at the hotel [Cameron's] saw Marks. My aunt intended to pass the winter at Santa Clara."

The two story Science Building with its handsome cupola was completed in 1861 and located southwest of the Mission Church. In the same year [1861], Father Burchard Villiger, S.J., who supervised its construction also directed the construction of a new brick facade and two towers on the Church front.

November 27.

"Thanksgiving day—This morning we were allowed to sleep till half past six. The greatest, or at least the most worth thing to be remarked, is the dinner we had today. The turkeys were very good, at least the one I carved, the tables were well supplied with different kinds of dishes. The best part of the dinner were the desserts, Floating Islands, pies, cakes, wine, etc. At half past three or there abouts, we went walking, went towards San Jose, stopped at Beaty's to see a pigeon match. Some excellent shots were made by a few, from Beaty's we came back to the College, we had no study in the whole day, and this evening I was very busy preparing my different lessons and exercises."

Two ugly events took place in San Jose during November 1862. The first was when a young Californian was found murdered. The culprit was captured and immediately placed in jail with iron shackles about his ankles, but when the case came to trial, the judge decided that it was justifiable homicide. A second unpleasant scene took place in one of San Jose's hotels when a bitter dispute between two stage drivers was finally ended when a ghastly knife wound resulted in the death of one driver. These and various minor crimes prompted Father Caredda to stop all visits to the settlement unless the students had been invited to visit a relative or a prominent citizen at Crandell's Hotel. At no time were they to loiter about San Jose.

Sunday, November 30.

"This morning I went to communion, few boys went. . . . two boys were admitted as Sodalists, John Hyde and Guerin. Shaffner was rejected for his being too young. This evening I had to study even more my astronomy also the rest of my class lessons. During the whole day I was not once in the yard. The whole of the day continued cloudy giving appearance of rain but none fell and so passed the month of November without a drop of rain."

15

The Close of 1862

On December 4, after J.M. had written a long letter to Mr. Ward, he called upon Dona Soledad Ortega de Arguello to express his sympathy upon the recent death of her brother-in-law, Santiago Arguello. Don Santiago Arguello died at Rancho La Tia Juana on November 9, 1862; six years after the demise of his son, Santiago Emigdio of La Puente. J.M. then went to San Jose and towards evening, returned to the college on the omnibus which ". . . was crowded with boys. There were four ladies inside, and of course they took most of the room with their hoops."

Because hoops were very fashionable during this period, a merchant near Santa Clara's Cameron Hotel frequently displayed large sets of them on the wooden sidewalk in front of his establishment. He stacked the varied-sized hoops in such a manner that the display gave the appearance of large bee-hives. They were so popular during the Civil War period that even piano stools were made about the size of a pie-tin, enabling ladies to seat themselves gracefully by giving a slightly circular lift of their hooped skirts, which quickly covered the plush-covered stool without exposing their ankles. It was not uncommon for gentlemen to step into gutters to make room for ladies wearing exceptionally large hoops.

When J.M. returned to the college, one of the students informed him that his name had been placed on the list of boys to be questioned in regard to the package that had been thrown into the garden of the San Jose Convent. J.M. was astounded. That the Fathers suspected him of having been one of the offenders was incredible. Because no further mention of this appears in his 1862 journal, one may presume strong

143

action took place upon the opening of the 1863 semester. To date, J.M.'s journal of that year has not been located.

December 5.

"Today it was my turn to fast, that was if I wished to do it, not obliged—had no breakfast, at dinner I ate a piece of pie, and at supper I took the usual meal. We had a very cold morning. We began nomenclature in chemistry. I heard from Duffy last night that Keating had married Lizzie Miller, at Washoe. I would not believe it at first, but he assured me it so much that I believe the marriage did take place. This evening I was very busy making an analysis of the three sentences for tomorrow. Besides Father Neri, I do not think I spoke to any other Father on the whole day, so much is my heart loaded with grief to think that at least two or three of them have so much suspicion against me for what occurred first Thursday before last. This evening Father Caredda came into the study room and spoke to us about the violation of some rules, or at least they were not observed as they should. He mentioned the following places with several remarks to each; Chapel, wash-room, study room, class room, Silence not kept after prayers, etc. Infirmary, no one aloud [sic] to visit anyone without special permission. The ranges not well kept. Dormitory silence not kept. A few remarks about first Thursday, the people at San Jose were displeased with many boys in the way they acted. This evening there was a total eclipse of the moon. It commenced at thirty five minutes to eleven. We were in bed at the time, but I had reminded Father Prelatto to wake me up when it would begin to eclipse, for we anticipated it before we went to bed; it was already announced in the *Alta* today. We remained in the yard around a large fire till 25 minutes after eleven. Father Nattini treated us with candy. We were with him, only six boys, viz, Delmas, Bowie, Marks, Townsend, Behan and myself."

Father Caredda demanded gentlemanly behavior at all times, particularly when students visited Santa Clara or San Jose. He also disapproved of untidiness in the dormitory where each student was assigned a section of the "Toilet Room" for his exclusive use. Each had a small cupboard, wash-basin, bowl, boot-stool, and a towel-rack, but students were obliged to provide for their own soap and polish for their boots.

December 6.

"I saw in the Morning *Call* an article where it said that the chief squatter of San Leandro has at length given up the fight against the family. This

I presume is Mulford and that he purchased one thirty-sixth of the ranch for $10,000 in coin which he delivered to Mr. Ward. From home I have not received any news, but it is very probably that such may have been the case."

The item J.M. read in San Francisco's *Morning Call* could lead some to the conclusion that the controversies between Mr. J.W. Mulford and the Estudillos were brought to a close with his purchase of a portion of Rancho San Leandro. However, in 1867, the smoldering ashes of troubles and ill-feelings again burst into flame. J.M.'s *Journal for 1867* bears one of the many difficulties that arose. On October 7, 1867 he wrote: "This morning Mr. Ward, Mr. Cushing (husband of Dolores Estudillo) and ourselves, that is my brothers, including Jose Antonio, who arrived this morning, and all the ranch hands, repaired to the warehouse for the purpose of taking out straw that Mulford had piled inside, which occupied nearly half of the warehouse. We all worked hard during the forenoon and continued again in the afternoon, when Mulford and his squatter friends, Wicks, Smith, Cummings, and six or seven men arrived in wagons. We were at our work clearing the bails [*sic*] out of the warehouse. Mulford jumped from his wagon and said that he came there for a row, when Mr. Ward approached him and told him that we would have it now. Mulford walked towards the door of the warehouse and tried to prevent the straw being taken out by different threats, when Mr. Ward took him by the coat and told him to mind his own business and get out of the way. Several crowded around. Then, when Mulford made a sign as to draw a weapon, Jose Antonio caught him by the hand. After a good deal of talk, Mulford started for the double-barrel shot guns which he said he had at his home. We continued to take Mulford's straw out until six o'clock when Sheriff Morse arrived with a writ for our arrest. We all crowded around to hear the accusation. It was issued for the malicious destruction of Mr. T.W. Mulford's grain. We all came to town and appeared before Justice Smith and pleaded not guilty. Griffith took our case. Mr. Nugent was present. We were left to go on our personal declaration of appearing here tomorrow." On the following day, J.M. wrote: "The whole of this day was spent in the trial of Mr. Mulford's suit. The Justice occupied the supervisor's room. The most barefaced swearing took place. Smith swore that he did not know that Mr. Ward had been put in possession of the 17-18 warehouse. Smith is a partner of Mulford's, one who had to pay the costs in the suit that put us in possession. We were discharged, as the complaint failed to prove that we had done any malicious injury to Mr. Mulford's straw. We brought in a suit for riotous attempt and the carrying of concealed weapons; but for the miserable behavior of the District Attorney, would have convicted them of both charges, but they were also dismissed."

December 8.

"Went to communion. This day eight years ago, one of the great dogmas of our Catholic Religion was openly declared in Rome in a seat Council where Pope Pius the IX, with many cardinals, Archbishops, bishops, priests, and articles or our Faith, this was the Immaculate Conception, pronounced to be pure Virgin mother of Christ. For ages she has been so. Sodality being under her patronage, today we celebrated with all the pomp of a great festival. A new member was admitted as Sodalist, Guerrin. This should be a holy day to all the United States. She has been put under the protection of the Blessed Virgin. This evening the sodality had their treat, only Sodalists were present. I was called to give a toast which I did. After supper we (only students) had a dance in the small study room."

December 10.

"This evening after the first study, all the members of the Sodality were called to the chapel with the exception of Bowie, Roche, Marks and Duffy. The object of the meeting was explained by the President, the substance of which I'll endeavor to set down. He explained to us how much must have been the displeasure of the Blessed Virgin and God himself incurred by a secret oath which was made by the above names already mentioned, they belonging to a secret Society in this College, joined with three or four others. Their names were taken from the register of the Sodality and burnt [sic] before the alter, before us, before God. The President remarked that their names were not worthy of remaining in the Sodality. The two assistants elected in the place of Bowie and Roche, I, first Assistant, Valenzuela the second, with some remarks the President concluded and we went back to the study room."

Secret meetings or the forming of secret societies were absolutely forbidden. No student abided by or grieved more over infractions of college rules than J.M., especially if any of his friends or classmates were involved. "Bowie" was Augustus J. Bowie and a member of a prominent San Francisco family. In the following year, Bowie received the first diploma issued by San Francisco's St. Ignatius College.

December 11.

"I heard from Father Guerrini some of the secret designs of the secret Society carried in this College, he said that in the writing now in the possession of the President, they had resolved that in the next meeting the company (cadets) would have to insult either the Captain or the 1st Lieutenant by striking him. I am indeed astonished to see how much hypocrisy could have been carried on by the leader of such a Society. Today the weather was rainy, I am suffering at present from a bad cold. This afternoon after study, Faure, Delmas, Valenzuela, Vallejo and myself went into a class room and had some sardines cakes, pies, etc. Hughes came in afterwards, we had a first rate time."

December 12.

"This morning the 'honorable gentleman,' Mr. Bowie, left the College and Marshall Hastings is about to leave. These two are the principal leaders of the Society they established. The weather today was tempetous [*sic*], a terrible north wind blew all day. We began a new set of books for bookkeeping. I subscribed for the *Scientific American* for the past two and for the ensuing year. In a conversation with Father Neri I learnt more things about the doings of the secret society."

December 13.

"Wrote a letter to Mr. Ward, sent it to San Jose by the Omnibus, there to be left at the stage office so that it would start tomorrow by the Oakland stage. After astronomy class I went into one of the classrooms with Father Prelatto and read the office of the Sodality in Latin. In Natural Philosophy we had explained the three different kinds of pumps, viz, common suction pump, the forcing pump, and the pressing pump. In my letter to Mr. Ward I asked him to send me ten dollars to defray my expenses going home next Monday week."

December 15.

"Received this afternoon a letter from Lola, dated the 5th inst., she tells me that she sends me a mocking bird, in return she wants me to send her the canary bird I promised her, and also a Christmas present and sundry little things. I received a hat, fits me well, also the *Sacramento Union*. I had a conversation with Van Ness what Father Caredda had spoken to him some time ago about what was thrown into the Convent with the name of G.R. (Grace Ida Riddle) attached to it. I inquired what it was that

Father C. said to him about me. He said that Father Caredda had told him that he had spoken to me and that I denied everything. Now what F. Caredda asked me, was if I had seen any of the boys in the vicinity of the Convent, or day scholars. I told him 'no,' then he asked me with whom such and such a boy was with most of the time. This I answered to the best of my knowledge, Van Ness told him that I was perfectly innocent, which is the very truth."

December 16.

"I am anxious of receiving an answer from Mr. Ward and know if he is going to send me the small sum (ten dollars) I asked for to be forwarded to me for my traveling expenses. This morning it was one of the coldest mornings of the session, the roofs were covered with frost. This afternoon Roche left the College . . . Roche was shamefully expelled after having promised to break all connections with the said society, he now continues to carry on their plans, he writes to Hastings to know what to do, that everything has remained idle and no steps were taken to continue its renewal. The letter fell into the hands of the President and the consequences were his expulsion."

On December 17, J.M. wrote a letter to Stephen Smith, of Bodega, California, all the details of the secret society, its members, resolutions, and the expulsion of his friends, mainly Bowie and Hastings of San Francisco. On the following day, he had a long conversation with his friend, Cook, a one-time member of the secret society who said he was indeed sorry that he joined it and that ". . . Hastings said at the Convent the he, Cook, had left the society only for cowardice, and it was rumored that the members wished to give him a good whipping when out of College." In 1862 and 1863, three Cook brothers of San Francisco attended Santa Clara College. These were Sydney, Herman and Walter.

December 20.

"I went to confession. In English class we had declamation. I spoke Patrick Henry's speech 'the war inevitable.' We had quite an interesting class in astronomy, we learnt how to find out when the moon would be full of new moon, also how to find out the golden number and also the Epact. This afternoon we had a literary entertainment in the theater. Some speeches, a dialogue, a lecture on oxygen by Cook, reading of the Salamagundi papers, music by the band, etc. There were no strangers . . .

"We were up this morning at half past six A.M., had breakfast and went to the steamboat stage office, it rained at the time very hard. With some trouble we managed to get our seats in one of the stages, drove to the convent and there my friends' sisters got in, also Miss Hastings. The coach was crowded almost to suffocation, but the presence of so many ladies in it was exceedingly pleasing. As we were about to leave town, many ladies crowded around to get their passage in our coach, but we would not give our seat. All this time it rained in torrents, but soon cleared off and we had a pleasant trip to the [Alviso] boat where we arrived at half past eight or nine A.M. Soon after our arrival, the stage from Santa Clara arrived with the boys and the Fathers that accompanied us in the boat, they were the President, Father Villiger, Father Caredda, Father Guerrin. Also Mr. Pascal, a lay teacher, came. The boat was late in leaving Alviso, there was a large crowd on board and good deal of freight. On board I had a pleasant time, passed most of the time in the parlor conversing with the young ladies. Cook introduced me to Miss Hastings. I found Miss Faure quite an accomplished young lady, we made a very slow trip, we arrived at the city [San Francisco] at two or half past.

December 23.

"I awoke this morning very early and at half past five A.M. we had a severe shock, its intensity was sufficient to awaken all but the very hardest sleepers. Its vibrations lasted about twenty seconds. It shook the house very much, the door of my room was opened." William H. Brewer was in San Francisco during the earthquake and wrote: "Three shocks followed in quick succession, the whole lasting not over six or eight seconds. The first awakened me, and with it came a slight nausea. The bed seemed lifted, then it shook and the house rocked, not as if jarred by the wind but as if heaved on some mighty wave, which caused everything to tremble as it was being heaved." Brewer added that it was the most severe earthquake San Francisco had experienced during the past seven years. [W.H. Brewer, *op. cit.*, p. 358.]

San Francisco. December 24.

"This morning I wrote a letter to Lola and another to Jose Antonio Arguello on the business concerning shingles I sent to San Diego. I sent them by the steamer 'Senator,' three boxes of different things, many little things besides; it kept me busy all day preparing them for the steamer. I saw the new hall where the church (St. Ignatius) will be opened tomorrow. I promised to come and visit the hall building tomorrow. This evening I went to bed very late, did not go out after supper. I wish you all health, happiness and cheer, a jovial Christmas and a happy year."

December 25.

"Welcome Mary [*sic*] Christmas! I was up this morning very early. I went to leave some letters on board the 'Senator,' came home (to the Nugents') and got ready to go to church which was at eleven A.M. I went to the choir, it was at St. Ignatius in the new hall. Father Bushard preached, most of the sermon was read. I saw all the Fathers from Santa Clara. After church I went to visit Barry Hyde, he was not at home, I saw his father and mother. I found Mrs. Hyde a very accomplished lady; after I had left the house I found Barry on the street. I met many school mates. This evening after supper I went to the Tehema House to see Leese, (Jack Leese, Jr.) but did not see him; coming out I met Grace Riddle and J.Y. (John Young), another gentleman and lady. I spoke to them, but not until Young called me. I went to the theater at the Metropolitan. Grace was there, also, Thomas Duffy . . ."

The gayest of the winter season's theater parties assembled to enjoy Mr. J.B. Booth, the celebrated actor, appearing in *The Chain of Guilt,* a drama that commanded undivided attention throughout the performance. San Francisco's billboards and periodicals also advertised the *Mammoth Minstrel and Vaudeville Company* and the appearance of the celebrated harpist and tenor, Señor Abecco, at Maguire's Opera House. J.M. probably felt self-conscious, lonesome, and somewhat uncomfortable upon seeing charming and beautifully gowned young ladies in the company of his friends. His uneasiness mounted when "Grace Riddle sent John Young to ask me if I knew who it was that wrote a letter to her that had fallen into the hands of the Sisters (at the Convent of Notre Dame), of course I not knowing who was the perpetrator, answered that I did not know. I went out of the theater before everything was over, went to look for Leese but he was not in his room. Came to the Russ House, found Mr. F. Ward, played two games at billiards and retired to rest." [J.M. probably left the theater early to avoid being embarrassed further by questions which led him to believe that Miss Riddle may have thought that he was one of the offenders.]

The sun shone gloriously in San Francisco during the Christmas season, but the nights were bitter cold and mornings found a thin coating of ice in the gutters. The *Daily Alta California* of December 26, bears the following account of the city's festivities while the diarist wandered about in search of companionship and walked many miles as an errand boy for Messrs. Orr and Ward: "There were a great many public and private dinner parties in the evening, and soirees in some of the principal hotels and in the citizens' mansions . . . There were hundreds who patronized the cars and stages running to the 'Willows.' The city was decorated with flags, countless lengths of garlands and other Christmas decorations and every church was filled to capacity." San Leandro was equally festive. Candle-lighted Christmas sparkled behind lace curtains through the settlement, particularly in the ornate, Victorian homes along 'The Avenue.' Even the smallest shops were decorated. San Leandro's 'Barber and Expert Tooth-Puller' had sprays of toyon berries in a large jar at his front window and near it, a smaller jar filled with extracted teeth which was always on display to prove his unique skill. Enterprising boys of the settlement had gathered great branches of laurel trees, some eight to ten feet in height, which they had sold to merchants for 25 to 50 cents apiece. These were tied to hitching posts in front of their establishments.

According to Mr. F. Eber of San Leandro, the great laurel branches that had decorated the various business establishments were taken down and dragged to the Plaza in front of the *Estudillo House*. At midnight the great pile was ignited amidst rejoicing throngs, the blowing of innumerable horns and whistles and the tolling of church bells to welcome the New Year. [Personal interview with the late Mr. F. Eber in 1938.]

Although J.M. went to the Tehema House on the northwest corner of California and Sansome Streets in San Francisco to visit this friend, Jacob Leese, Jr., his greatest hope was that Miss Riddle would be seated in the parlor with her parents. It always pleased him greatly when he occasionally met her on her way or leaving the offices of "J.L. Riddle & Company—Real Estate and Auctioneers" at 523 Montgomery Street. It was considered exceedingly improper for unmarried young people to converse on the streets even momentarily unless the young lady was accompanied by her parents or an adult known to the young man. Miss Riddle never stopped to speak to the diarist, which was expected, but if she merely bowed her pretty head in recognition, it was worth the sauntering back and forth along Montgomery Street. Most gratifying to him was when this charming young lady softly said 'Mr. Estudillo' as he bowed and tipped his hat in passing.

"This evening there was a great deal of talking about the 'Alabama' having captured the small steamer from New York to Aspinwall. I went to bed at half past eight o'clock." William H. Brewer heard the same report while in San Francisco and on the following day he wrote; "All the city is in great excitement over the capture of the California steamer 'Ariel' by the British pirate 'Alabama,' or '290.'" [W.H. Brewer, *op. cit.*, p. 359.]

San Leandro. December 28.

"I was awakened by Vicente this morning at six A.M. Last night I had intended to go to the city on the first boat, but seeing the state of the weather, which was not at all pleasant, I determined to wait till the second boat. I left San Leandro at ten minutes after nine, passing by Mr. [Joseph M.] Dillon's house, I caught up with Mrs. Cronley, Clara and Miss Lucy Lee, spoke with Mrs. Cronley. I drove to the stable, left the buggy and walked to church.

"After Mass I went to the stable, took a ride out to the railroad track." [The tracks were those of the *San Francisco and Oakland Ferry Railroad Company* being lain from Broadway along 7th Street to the Oakland pier, a distance of four miles. The railroad-ferry project was commenced on August 2, 1862, although the company had been granted the right-of-way along 7th Street to the bay on November 20, 1861. On September 2, 1863, the first locomotive was put into operation along this route.]

"I came back in time for the boat, passed to the city (San Francisco) on the half past two boat. This evening I went to Vespers, the church was crowded as usual. Father Buchard gave his instructions on the seventh commandment. As I was coming from the boat, who would I meet on Montgomery Street, but her majesty, Miss Grace Riddle, the usual bow of course I made. Went to bed at half past twelve."

Once again, he bowed to Miss Riddle, but despite her indifference, his pride rarely permitted a manifestation of his injured feelings even in his strictly private journals. In 1864, he was greatly offended by a sudden indifferent attitude on the part of a particularly charming young lady, after he had escorted her home from a social function. Before retiring he vented his feelings by writing: "Nay, if she loves me not, I care not for her; shall I look pale because the maiden blooms? Or sigh because she smiles, and smiles on others? Not I, by Heaven!! I hold my peace too dear, to let it, like the plumes upon her cap, shake at each nod that caprice shall dictate."

J.M. may have been more at ease and less lonely had he remained at

Santa Clara College, which was his privilege even though the fall semester had closed. His restlessness may have been due, in part, to an unconscious longing for the companionship and paternalistic kindness of the Fathers. At the college he undoubtedly would have placed evergreens in the ancient chapel, lighted candles and escorted the aged to their pews. Such assignments had always created a sense of great comfort by being a part of the Father's sacred work. The strong bond that had been formed between him and his instructors is exemplified by a notation in his *Journal for 1864* during his last session at the institution. It reads: "A week ago I was in San Leandro and left there on Friday also. Immediately on getting up, a thought came to my mind, which was what I did at home after getting up—how I walked through the garden and enjoyed its beautiful flowers, and the fruit trees loaded with fruit, and now, here I was going down to the washroom and wash myself; a little patience and all this will be over, and I will have a good deal of home life; not that I will ever regret my College time. This is a thought which I think of, it wounds my heart, and now that I am to enter the busy world, I feel as if some paterli [sic] linked me to the College. I feel that I cannot leave. Tho my course in life be a happy one, I will never recall happier and sweeter days than my College time. And since I have entered into this declaration of my feelings, I will cite at length, some particulars and let the names of Reverend Fathers Caredda, Cicaterri, former President, Reverend Veyret, my confessor, Father Prelatto, Reverend B. Villiger, President; my former professor, Mr. Pascal, together with College companions with me into the farthest corner of which the four winds may happen to throw me. And there, be as dear to me as they always were. My friends, two more months and I will bid you farewell . . . fare thee well long-loved spot. No more, no more shall I be enclosed within those classic halls. May prosperity always be with you."

William H. Brewer was also equally lonely in San Francisco during the Christmas season in 1862. He wrote: "I cannot divest my mind and memory of the association of this season with snowy landscapes and tinkling sleigh bells, and leafless forests. I find a feeling of sadness akin to homesickness creeping over me, that my fireside seems more desolate than ever, and my path in life a lonelier one." [*op. cit.,* pp. 359-360.] Had Brewer remained in his beloved mountains and country-side studying the formations, flora and other wonders of nature, and J.M. at neighboring Santa Clara, each would have found solace in their separate fields.

San Francisco. December 29.

"Soon after breakfast Mr. Ward and myself walked to the office on Front Street. I was quite busy in the office this afternoon. I had to arrange the papers on the ranch and separating the private letters from the business ones, putting the bills paid, etc. in their right places. I took two or three trips to the house (Nugent's home). I saw Miss Grace on Montgomery Street three or four times, the last, I spoke to her. I was promised a New Year's present by Mr. Ward of a watch, did not get it today, but hope I shall get it tomorrow. I waited at the office for Mr. Ward since two P.M. till quarter after four, he did not come thereupon I shut the office and came home. I met Father Neri in the street. On the way I met Juan and Murphy, had a drink at the bar of the Lick House and then walked to the house (the Tehema House Hotel). I went to bed this evening very late."

December 31.

"This morning I went to church. James Hughes and myself this afternoon went over to Oakland on the half past two boat. I invited him to go. I went for the purpose of bringing over to the city, Mr. Ward's mares. At Oakland we took a ride around town, came over on the last boat, it was rather late when we arrived in the city. James rode with me as far as the corner of Washington and Montgomery, thence I drove to the stable on the Fourth Street. After supper I went to St. Ignatius to hear the hymn in thanksgiving. From Church I went to town, walked to Sherwood's Jewelry store. I got a watch and chain made a present to me by Mr. Ward. I met Reichert and we walked together for awhile. We stopped for a long time at Platt's Hall. A ball was given for the benefit of the female orphans on Market Street. I had not the least idea of going though I wanted to see Barry Hyde."

Platt's Hall was a large, three-story building erected in 1860, on the corner of Montgomery and Bush Streets. The benefit was for the Roman Catholic Orphan Asylum; also known as Mount St. Joseph's School for Girls, organized in 1852, and incorporated in 1858. The institution educated and cared for orphan girls between the ages of five years and nine months and eighteen years.

"I came home at quarter to twelve, when at the house I made up my mind to go to the hall. Got ready and started. At the ball, I met Hyde, I was introduced to Miss O'Neil, had three dances with her which was all I danced. I did not have any other acquaintances and so did not dance. I was very much tired when everything was over although I did not dance much. I came home (the hotel) with Reichert and went to bed at five o'clock A.M. That is the way I passed the old year out and welcomed the new. Let us be marry [*sic*] when the old year dies, Let us extol the New Year to the skies."

Epilogue

With this admonition end the journals of Jesus Maria Estudillo. A century and a quarter have passed since the final entry. Few of the landmarks he described remain today except as names of places and streets.

Estudillo would find it hard to believe the changes that have taken place: his family's *Rancho San Leandro* is now almost solid city; the stagecoach roads are freeways, and a trip from San Francisco to Los Angeles takes an hour or two by jet instead of days by steamer.

Today's young people will be amused by the restrictions of etiquette by which his generation was bound and he would be equally disturbed to see their freedom. But his marriage to a divorced Protestant, mentioned on page 35, "a heartbreak greater than death," may have been his way of breaking with the social restrictions with which he had been bound throughout his younger years.

Jesus Maria Estudillo has passed into obscurity except for his diaries, saved by the daughter of the divorceé he married. From her friend Ynez Tillinghest, who became Ynez Estudillo following her mother's marriage, Margaret Schlichtmann learned of the journals and borrowed them to read. Thus began this account. The diaries now repose safely for posterity in the Bancroft Library at the University of California in Berkeley.

Genealogy

This genealogy wase compiled in part from baptismal records of Missions Carmel, San Diego, San Francisco de Asis (Dolores), Santa Clara, Santa Barbara and San Jose and from baptismal records of Saint Leander's Church, San Leandro, California and from baptismal records of Saint Mary's Church in Oakland, California. Additional data were acquired from Matrimonial Records of the Presidio Church of Santa Barbara, Mission San Francisco de Asis (Dolores) and the church of the Royal Presidio of Monterey. Other sources are:

Biographical Files, San Diego Historical Society, San Diego, California.

Biographical Files, Santa Barbara Historical Society, Santa Barbara.

B.I. Hayes, *Notes on California Affairs* and *Reminiscences,* Bancroft Library, University of California, Berkeley, California.

H.H. Bancroft, *History of California,* Vol. II, III, IV.

J.M. Estudillo, *Journals for 1861, 1862, 1864, 1867,* Bancroft Library.

J.M. Estudillo, Biographical Notes (undated) in possession of writer.

Winifred Davidson's *Notes,* San Diego Historical Society.

San Diego Census, June 8, 1860, San Diego Historical Society.

R.W. Bracket, *The History of San Diego County Ranches.*

W.H. Davis, *Sixty Years in California.*

Proceedings of Land Case No. 256, N.D. U.S. District Court, San Francisco. Bancroft Library.

Grace Carmel Martinez, *Don Ignacio Martinez—Illustrous Pioneer.*

Union Title—Trust Topics, Vol. IV., No. 6, November-December 1950. San Diego, California.

Children of Don José María Estudillo y Gomez (1772-1830) and his wife, Aña María Gertrudis de Horcasitas y Herrera.

1. Bernavela, Joaquina, Antonia, Maria, Ignacia. June 11, 1799, Mon-

terey Presidio. Carmel Mission Baptismal Records (1770-1820) June 11, 1799, Vol. I., Entry No. 2279.

2. Joaquin, Antonio, Jose, Ygnacio, Fernando, Ramon, Pio V. (Pope Pius V., 1572) Monterey Presidio, May 5, 1800. Mission Carmel Baptismal Records, Vol. I., Entry No. 2308. (This was Don Jose Joaquin Estudillo, grantee of Rancho San Leandro.)

3. Maria, Francisca del Rosario, Gertrudis, Agustina, Antonia, Josefa. October 9, 1801, Monterey Presidio. Mission Carmel Records, Vol. I., Entry No. 2376.*

4. Jose, Antonio, Ramon, Joaquin, Ignacio, Victorino. September 2, 1803, Monterey Presidio. Mission Carmel Records, Vol. I., Entry No. 2445.

5. Maria, Dolores, Damiana. May 26, 1805, Monterey Presidio. Mission Carmel Records, Vol. I., Entry No. 2504.

6. Maria del Carmen, Clara, Ramona, Pia. May 4, 1807, Monterey Presidio, Mission Carmel Records, Vol. I., Entry 2640.

7. Maria, Guadalupe, Jacoba, Eugenia, November 27, 1812, Monterey Presidio. Mission Carmel Records, Vol. I., Entry No. 2862.

8. Maria, Magdalena, 1815.

9. Maria, Antonia

The Mission Record of June 11, 1799, signed by Fray Fermín Francisco Lasuen gives "Horcasitas" as the surname of Ana Maria Gertrudis, but in the record of May 5, 1800 and signed by Fray Jacinto Lopez, it is spelled "Orcasitas." Variations in spelling appear in other Mission records.

* The translated baptismal record Entry No. 2376 and dated October 9, 1801, and signed by Fray Jose Vinals bears in part ". . . a little girl born the fourth legitimate child of Don Jose Maria Estudillo. . . ." Unless a child was born in Mexico prior to the Estudillos' arrival in California, 1801 marks the birth of their third child and not their fourth. The three earliest children born in Monterey arrived in 1799, 1800, and 1801. The fourth, a son, was born in 1803.

Children of Don José Joaquin Estudillo (1800-1852) and his wife, Juana María del Carmen Martinez (1805-1879)

1. Marí de la Concepcíon, Francisca, April 14, 1824. San Francisco

Presidio. Mission Dolores Baptismal Records, Book 2., Entry No. 364.

2. José, Romanus, Francisco, Antonio, Ramon, February 8, 1827. San Francisco Presidio. Mission Dolores Baptismal Records, Book 2., Entry No. 398.
3. María de Jesús, Telesfora de los Reyes, January 5, 1829, San Diego Presidio, Mission San Diego Baptismal Records, Vol. 2., Entry 6255.
4. José, Antonio, Dario, December 20, 1830. San Diego Presidio. Mission San Diego Baptismal Records, Vol. 2., Entry No. 6392.
5. José, María, January 20, 1833. Pueblo San José de Rio Guadalupe.
6. José, Vicente, February 19, 1834, Pueblo San José de Rio Guadalupe.
7. Ladislaus, Dennis, Luís. October 1836, El Rancho Pinole. Mission Dolores Baptismal Records, Book 2., Entry No. 7054.
8. María, Filomena de Guadalupe, July 5, 1838. El Rancho Pinole. Mission Dolores Baptismal Records, Book 2., Entry No. 7099. She died on January 21, 1850.
9. María, Dolores, Gertrudis. April 15, 1840. Rancho San Leandro. Mission San José Baptismal Records, (Nov. 22, 1830-May 8, 1859) Entry No. 7481.
10. María, Magdalena de la Encarnacion, Veneranda. April 1842, Rancho San Leandro. Mission San José Baptismal Records, Entry No. 8172.
11. Jesús María de la Trinidad, June 29, 1844, Rancho San Leandro. Mission San José Baptismal Records, Entry No. 8312. This was the diarist of *Journals for 1861, 1862, 1864 and 1867*. His godparents were Victor Castro and Guadalupe Moraga.

Children of Jose Antonio Estudillo (1803-1852) and his wife, Maria Victoria Domínguez (1801-1851)

1. Maria, Antonia. September 27, 1826, San Diego Presidio. Mission San Diego Baptismal Records, Vol. 2, Entry No. 6061.
2. Maria Francisca, About October 1827, San Diego.
3. Maria del Rosario, September 2, 1828. San Diego, Mission San Diego Baptismal Records, Vol. 2, Entry No. 6234.
4. Maria Luisa, August 11, 1830. San Diego. Mission San Diego Baptismal Records, Vol. 2., Entry No. 6369. According to this record her godfather was to be Don Juan Bandini, "who because of his absence gave his proxy to his father, Don Jose Bandini."
5. Maria de los Reyes, 1835, San Diego. Died in 1865.

6. Salvador de los Ramon, April 1, 1836, San Diego. Mission San Diego Baptismal Records, Vol. 2., Entry No. 6719.
7. Jose de Guadalupe, Concepcion, February 3, 1838, San Diego. Mission San Diego Baptismal Records, Vol. 2., Entry No. 6870.
8. Maria, Concepcion, 1843. San Diego.
9. Francisco Maria, July 23, 1844, San Diego. Mission San Diego Baptismal Records, Vol. 2., Entry No. 7063.
10. José Maria, named in honor of his paternal grandfather.

Children of Ygnacio Martinez de la Vega (1774-1848) and his wife, Maria, Martina Ramirez de Arellanes (1788-?)
1. Maria Antonia, 1803, Santa Barbara Presidio.
2. Juana Maria del Carmen, November 30, 1805. Santa Barbara Presidio.
3. Maria de Encarnacion, 1807.
4. Jose Antonio.
5. Jose de Jesus Ciriaco, about 1816.
6. Jose Vicente Ramon, August 18, 1818. Santa Barbara Presidio.
7. Susana, March 21, 1824.
8. Francisca, March 21, 1824.
9. Rafaela, April 17, 1826.
10. Maria Luisa, 1828, San Francisco Presidio.
11. Maria Concepcion Ygnacia, August 3, 1829. San Francisco Presidio. Mission Dolores Baptismal Records, Vol. 2., Entry No. 424.
12. Maria Dolores, March 10, 1832, San Jose. Mission Santa Clara Baptismal Records, Book 2., Entry No. 8492.
13. Teniente, 1838.

Children of Juan Bandini (1800-1859) and his first wife, Maria de los Dolores Damiana Estudillo (1805-1833)
1. Maria Josefa Ramona Maximiana, August 22, 1823. San Diego Presidio. Mission San Diego Baptismal Records, Book 2., Entry No. 5520.
2. Alejandro Felix Rafael, November 20, 1824, San Diego Presidio. Mission San Diego Baptismal Records, Book 2., Entry No. 5846.
3. Maria Antonia Francisca de Paula, January 12, 1827. San Diego Presidio. Mission San Diego Baptismal Records, Book 2, Entry No. 6081.
4. Arcadia, San Diego.

5. Ysidora, San Diego.
6. Jose Maria, San Diego.
7. Juan Bautista Antonio de Padua, nicknamed "Juanito." November 5, 1833, San Diego. Mission San Diego Baptismal Records, Book 2, Entry No. 6576.

Children of Juan Bandini and his second wife, Refugia, daughter of Santiago Arguello, Sr.
1. Maria de los Dolores, San Diego.
2. Juan de la Cruz, San Diego.
3. Alfredo, San Diego.
4. Arturo, San Diego.
5. Dolores, San Diego.
6. Victoria, San Diego.
7. Margarita, nicknamed "Chata."

The last list of Don Juan Bandini's children is from the Biographical Files, *Bandini,* San Diego Historical Society, San Diego, California.

Children of Santiago (Santiaguito) Emigdio Arguello (1813-1857) and his wife, Maria, Guadalupe, Jacoba, Eugenia, Estudillo (1812-1880)
1. Josef, Dolores, December 3, 1837.
2. Francisco, late 1839, Rancho La Punta.
3. Maria, Gertrudis (nicknamed "Tula" or "Tulita,") July 8, 1840.
4. Maria del Refugia, Concepcion, April 26, 1842. (J.M. Estudillo *Journal For 1862,* Census of San Diego, 1860, see birthdate 1841.)
5. Maria, Antonia, 1844, La Punta.
6. Maria de los Dolores, Michaela, October 8, 1845. San Diego. Mission San Diego Baptismal Records, Book 2., Entry No. 7094.
7. Josef, Juan de la Cruz, March 2, 1851.
8. Maria Guadalupe.
9. Jose Ramon.

This list is not complete. Baptismal records of their other children have not been available to the writer of this account.

Children of Don Santiago Arguello (1792-1862) and his wife, Maria del Pilar Ortega (?-1878)

1. Santiago (Santiaguito) Emigdio. August 18, 1813, Santa Barbara Presidio.
2. Maria, Luisa, Married Don Augustin Vicente Zamorano in 1827.
3. Luis, Antonio, Early 1824.
4. Aloysius, Gonzaga Saturninus, November 9, 1824, San Diego Presidio. Mission San Diego Baptismal Records, Book 2., Entry No. 5848.
5. Maria de los Dolores, Agnes (or Ynez), April 18, 1826. San Diego Presidio. Mission San Diego Baptismal Records, Book 2., Entry No. 6013. Baptized, April 21, 1826.
6. Maria Antonia, 1844. La Punta or Rancho La Tia Juana.
7. José Ramón.
8. Maria Concepcion.

The Estudillo House stood at the corner of Davis Street and Washington Avenue in San Leandro. It was a popular meeting place before its destruction in 1929.

Broadway from the railroad station, Oakland, 1869

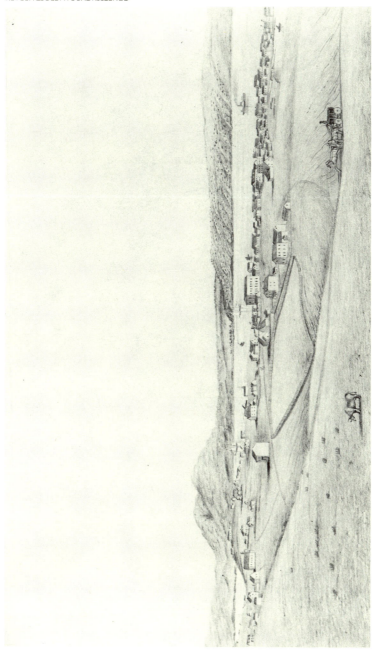

Benicia, California, in 1856, from a sketch by Henry Miller

165

Martinez, California, in 1856, from a sketch by Henry Miller

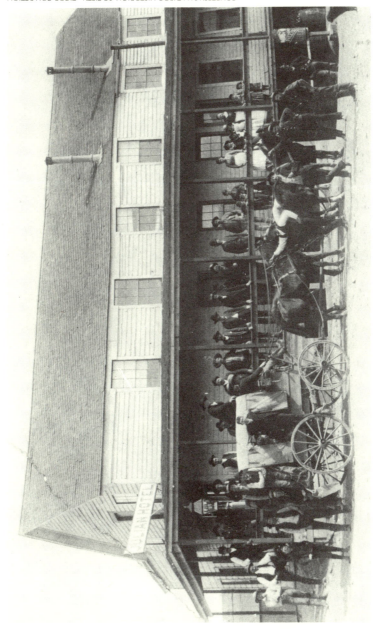

Julian Hotel, near San Diego about 1885. For four or less passengers, four horses were adequate (see p. 99).

The Cosmopolitan Hotel, where Estudillo stopped in Old Town San Diego, in 1872 (see p. 105).

Ruins of The Presidio, Old Town San Diego, about 1872 (see p. 105).

The sidewheeler SS *Orizaba*, photographed about 1888, was typical of the passenger vessels plying the California coast.

Rancho Guajome, located several miles south of San Luis Rey, was visited by Jesus Estudillo (see p. 122). Photographed in 1895.

Mr. and Mrs. Charles H. Cushing with children (from left) Thomas (born 1870), Elise (born 1865), Agnes (born 1874), and Charles (born 1866).

José Antonio Estudillo, brother of the diarist, Jesus.

Maria de Jesus Estudillo, sister of Jesus, married William Heath Davis, author of *60 Years in California*.

Mr. and Mrs. John B. Ward (Maria de la Concepcion, oldest sister of Jesus) with children Sophie Juana (born 1852), and John Francis (born 1859).

Juana Maria del Carmen Martinez de Estudillo, mother of Jesus Estudillo.

José Joaquin Estudillo, father of the diarist.

The University of Santa Clara, California, was founded in 1851. Old Mission Santa Clara stands at the left.

Jesus Estudillo sits on the steps of his home at 172 Estudillo Avenue, San Leandro. He died in 1910.

The Estudillo Mansion stood at the corner of Estudillo Avenue and Carpentier Street, San Leandro. Photographed about 1957.

SUNDAY, MARCH 23, 1862.

Second day of our Retreat, I passed most of time in the vineyard, except when I had to come and attend the exercises in the chapel or the study room. This afternoon from three o'clock to five we had no exercises in the chapel. I remained reading in the vineyard. The weather to-day has been incomparably lovely, no wind not dust in circulation, and the atmosphere was clear as crystal. After the terrible weather of last week, such days as the three past, with the present are to be appreciated. To-day I wrote a good deal of my letter to Mr Ward which I am writing this time in the study-room.

MONDAY 24

* Wrote a letter to Mr Ward. Third & last day of our Spiritual Retreat. And this evening I made a general confession, and during the recreations I had time to make a good examination of conscience in the vineyard. I was constantly meditating on these points: On hell and the glory of God, and of eternity, eternity, eternity. We had a rather disagreeable day. This afternoon I felt a little sick with sore throat, not of any danger. This day I shall mark as being one of the greatest to me, that is of having made up my good resolutions for the future; that the Retreat may not pass away without leaving some good impressions in my mind.

TUESDAY 25

* Received the ____ this morning
This morning I went to communion. As the B.dr preached us, he offered the mass. And this evening in state of vespers, again he gave us a last lecture. We had no school in the whole day, but on the afternoon I took my Atlas and Knapp's chemical Technology to make my lecture on artificial light, but I did very little, only wrote the Introduction. Roche was in the room also making his lecture. During the time I was there, J.y. came in and wished to speak to me, I came to the other room and told me that he wished me to tell O.P. to come to this room after the 2 o'k. mr. I did so with few words, this being the first time I had spoken to him since the 8th inst.

A page from the journal of Jesus Estudillo.

180